The
Bathroom
BOOK

The Bathroom
BOOK

Stylish transformations with paint, tiles, wood and glass

HENNY DONOVAN

APPLE

Contents

30 Blues and Lilacs

50 Aquas and Greens

First published in 2003 by
The Apple Press Ltd.
Sheridan House
112–116A Western Road
Hove
East Sussex
BN3 IDD

ISBN 1-84092-406-3

Conceived, designed and produced by
Quarto Publishing plc
The Old Brewery
6 Blundell Street
London N7 9BH

Editor Kate Tuckett
Senior Art Editor Sally Bond
Text Editors Jan Cutler, Gillian Kemp
Designer Julie Francis
Photographer Paul Forrester
Indexer Dorothy Frame

Art Director Moira Clinch
Publisher Piers Spence

Manufactured by Universal Graphics (Pte) Ltd., Singapore; printed by Star Standard Industries (Pte) Ltd., Singapore

▲ The stylish, graphic white and charcoal marble finishes in this bathroom have a clean, contemporary elegance with a timeless appeal. See pages 92–95.

INTRODUCTION

The bathroom is one of the most important rooms in the house in which to relax and rejuvenate. The general thrust of life these days is faster, busier and more demanding than ever before, and time to recharge and unwind is precious. It is hardly surprising that we want the space we have created for those rare moments to be a special retreat, somewhere that will cause a feeling of well-being as soon as we enter it; a space that restores the senses, makes us feel renewed and washes away the cares and stresses of the day. So the bathroom needs to look and feel good, which is why our focus has turned to its decoration and style. Decoration that is well thought out will create just the mood and atmosphere you want. *The Bathroom Book* will inspire you to try out a totally new decorating scheme, to create your own personal bathroom retreat.

The bathroom lends itself to a multitude of decorative possibilities: walls, panelling, floors, splashbacks, tiles, soft furnishings and bathroom furniture are all excellent surfaces to decorate. This potential, combined with a variety of different themes and techniques, provides all sorts of exciting possibilities for a completely new look.

The Bathroom Book brings these factors together into a new, easy-to-follow guide with 16 exciting and innovative step-by-step projects and 20 variations, all illustrated with inspirational photographs, to give you all the decorating ideas and know-how for a complete bathroom make-over in contemporary or updated classic styles.

Colour immediately alters the feeling and atmosphere of any room, making it at once invigorating, energizing, restful, calming or healing. With this in mind, the book has been organized by colour, each chapter demonstrating how to create the particular mood you want for your bathroom. An introductory section on colour is also included to give an insight into its uses.

Pattern is making a big comeback in the design and decoration of our homes. We are no longer content just with plain, minimalist walls, but seek the character, depth and interest that patterned surfaces create.

▶ Working with the thematic approach of New England style, palest grey wooden panelling and a shoreline border stencil, this bathroom has a light, fresh and clean feel. See pages 84–87.

► Warm, earthy terra-cotta shades are perfectly complemented by simple wooden accessories, giving this bathroom a rustic, old-world charm.

I have designed the stencils used throughout this book to show just how to bring pattern into a wide range of decorative schemes.

The projects illustrate how the extremely versatile decorative medium of design-based stencils in both modern and traditional pattern motifs can be applied to walls, floors, tiles, glass, fabrics and furniture. Stencilling has been used to create all-over pattern repeats, for example an 18th-century damask effect, as well as a modern, simple, geometric repeat. It has also been used to create a large koi carp mural in silver aluminium leaf, as well as for tile repeats on floors, beautiful spattered designs on tiles and mirror frames, subtle relief stencils and a faux mosaic splashback, as well as etched designs on glass, border repeats, and printed motifs on sheer fabrics.

I have also used a thematic approach for some of the bathrooms. Working with themes is great fun and can be one of the best ways to create a unified style. Theme-inspired projects include a modern Swedish style bathroom with thick wooden panelling and delicate printed fabrics, in a tone-on-tone monochromatic soft green colour scheme; a New England style retreat in tones of pale grey, ivory and blue-tinged charcoal, with a shoreline border and tongue-and-groove furniture and panelling (shown opposite); as well as Indian and Mediterranean style bathrooms. Other projects include a rich azure and ultramarine hand-painted seascape, cool Calacatta and limestone marble finishes, hand painted jewel-like tiles and metallic walls with etched glass squares.

Finishing and styling is essential to complete the look. Baths, sinks, basins, mirrors, taps and accessories – in sleek chrome, elegant glass, ceramic, marble and cast iron – are used throughout the bathroom sets to bring out the best in each design.

Before you start on your chosen bathroom effect, read the comprehensive introduction to planning and preparation to ensure your new, fantastic bathroom will be a stunning success, then go ahead and enjoy discovering *The Bathroom Book*.

GETTING STARTED

Planning the decorative scheme

In the last ten years the bathroom has become just as important a focus in the house as the main living areas. There is virtually no limit to the style and look that can be achieved, and there are extensive choices for bathroom fixtures in traditional styles and with sleek, modern lines. Options for bathroom accessories and fittings also seem to be endless – with comprehensive ranges in brushed or high-shine chrome, elegant glassware, porcelain, wood, rattan, bamboo, plastic and more. Such an extensive choice opens the door to many possibilities for new and complementary decorative schemes. So whether you are starting from scratch, with a completely new look, or planning a makeover to an existing bathroom, anything is possible.

STARTING POINTS

There are a number of useful starting points and inspirations to draw upon when choosing a decorative scheme. Use the following ideas to get you going and bring out the designer in you.

Inspired by a theme

Taking a thematic approach to designing a scheme can be extremely rewarding, great fun and one of the best ways to create a unified, holistic style, where the whole room and everything in it is brought together in the scheme. Sources for this might be cultural influences from the four corners of the globe, or specific period styles, or a combination of both.

◀ Rich, opulent pinks, purples and oranges with gold and glitter highlights blend perfectly in this Indian border motif for an Indian themed bathroom. See pages 104–107.

If New England style and the cool, bright, airy feeling of North Atlantic light inspire you, plan a whole theme around it. Old-world charm can be given a fresh, clean, modern feel, with wood painted in varying intensities of cool, neutral whites with splashes of colour. Add bleached wooden frames, soft neutral towels and all things natural, plucked from the outdoors.

If you love the exotic opulence of Indian fabrics, patterns, textures and colours, try this as a theme for a romantic bathroom. Several bright colours and intricate pattern motifs can be combined with rich silks, gold accents and dark, polished wood to create an exciting, yet intimate look.

Alternatively, try themes inspired by Mediterranean, Roman, French, Swedish or Oriental styles, or by the Medieval, Victorian, Neo-classical, Regency or Art Nouveau periods.

Inspired by mood or feelings

Modern day decoration, where we attempt to create particular feelings and moods, reflects the attitude we hold towards our homes and the way we live our lives. Colour is central to this. We know if we pick the right colour it will create a particular atmosphere. So we usually look at what we want to achieve first and then see which colour corresponds to this feeling; even when we choose the colour first there is an instinctive sense of what its effect will be. This is why colour choices are subjective and personal – based on feeling, rather than merely knowledge of the science of colour.

To create an atmosphere that will energize, stimulate and invigorate, choose intense and bright colours. But rather than painting a whole room with them, use them more like colour 'vitamins'. Use accents, accessories and splashes of intense colour, or perhaps paint just one wall.

To achieve a feeling of restfulness, balance and rejuvenation, use pastel colours. These will give a feeling of space and are most effective as solid blocks of colour, which produce a feeling of being bathed in the colour. Add accents of richer colours and natural materials to anchor the scheme (see Colour, pages 24–25).

Inspired by pattern

Pattern is integral to most design schemes: it gives depth and focus and is an excellent way of harmonizing colours. Most decorative schemes – apart from very minimalist designs – will have a pattern element, and even a plain-tiled bathroom has the geometric rhythm of the tiling itself.

Pattern falls roughly into four groups: geometric, motif, pictorial and floral. Each group can be used widely in schemes for the bathroom, either singly or repeated, large or small.

Geometric patterns produce a sense of order and can be used either in repeat on tiles, walls and floors or as strong features that will alter the feeling and proportion of a room – vertical stripes make rooms seem taller, horizontal stripes cause a space to appear wider.

A motif pattern can be either representational or abstract and can be used in diverse ways. It will link various elements of a room when used in repeat on different surfaces; or it can be featured on just one wall, or used as a border.

A pictorial pattern is generally representational and can be used very effectively on differing scales to create feature walls in the bathroom, such as on splashbacks or murals, or alternatively as an all-over repeat pattern.

Floral patterns create gentle detail and colour – modern interpretations of simple leaf motifs are an excellent example of this.

◄ Close-toned soft greens create a calming and restful mood. See pages 60–63.

▼ Large ornate floral motifs are used in this repeat pattern – a modern take on classic 18th-century floral wallpaper. See pages 40–43.

▲ Geometric – see pages 88–91

▲ Motif – see pages 72–75

▲ Pictorial – see pages 32–35

▲ Floral – see pages 64–67

◄ The four types of pattern – geometric, motif, pictorial, or floral – used either on their own or in repeated form, on small and large scales, create a complete matrix of pattern options.

Inspired by texture

There is an increasing demand for texture in our homes. We now consider texture as an integral part of decorative schemes, which gives tactile as well as visual possibilities. Shiny, smooth, silky and sleek sit quite happily alongside chalky, velvety, grained or coarse textures, whether on walls, floors, furniture or fabrics, or a host of complementary accessories. Textured surfaces work on their own or with smooth, contrasting elements, and are ideal for use in the bathroom.

Texture can be found in painted surfaces – when shiny and matt surfaces are combined – as well as in textured paints and coatings. Some paint finishes give the impression of texture, such as colourwashing, dragging, combing and distressing. Other paints are perfect for textured and relief effects such as impasto – where plaster paint or 3-D paint are applied thickly – and some have a built-in aggregate such as texture paint or suede paint (although suede paint is more suitable for a cloakroom than a bathroom). Plaster coatings, such as Italian marmorino or stucco lustro can be applied as a distressed or polished surface. And of course there are numerous textured wallpapers.

There are a variety of features to accompany these surfaces: the luxurious feel of cool, smooth marble, stone and natural minerals, the sleek lines of chrome and glass, and a host of metallic finishes whose lustre and reflective surfaces – whether in paint, varnish or gilded effects – all provide further possibilities for creating textural contrasts. The more obvious smooth, shiny bathroom fixtures, and the effective use of mirrors also offer countless textural opportunities of their own.

Inspired by technique

There are some techniques and finishes that have a character and look that stand in their own right as starting points for decorative schemes, and which work well in the bathroom setting.

Classical or modern mosaic might be the source of your inspiration: its texture, its feel and its pattern, constructed from many tiny segments of glass or ceramic. The specific decorative art form is the inspirational starting point here, with colour and design choices as secondary considerations. Mosaic can be cleverly emulated using stencils – whether on floors or walls – as a splashback, or decorative border.

Alternatively, you might find the effect of distressed painted panelling or a simple whitewashed floor particularly appealing – it's the appearance of the technique and the feeling that it creates that provides the inspiration. Otherwise, you may simply wish to create a marble bathroom, flexing your decorating muscles to design a unique, luxurious space.

▲ The texture of this distressed plaster effect, created using impasto or 3-D paint, is given extra lustre with the sheen of a metallic varnish and accessorized with a more subtly textured sleek, silver mirror. See page 69.

▶ Real mosaic is cleverly emulated in this dolphin mosaic stencil – perfect for a sink splashback; or create the look of a real limestone marble bathroom with this quality paint finish. See pages 56–59.

Room style and format

Abathroom can be a problem to plan imaginatively and effectively, simply because there are several large, fixed items that need to fit into a space that is often quite small, or an odd shape. All the plumbed-in features – such as the bathtub, sink, toilet and possibly a shower or bidet – are permanent. Whether you are planning an entirely new bathroom or a scheme around existing fixtures, they ultimately determine the space available for decorative work.

If you are designing this room from scratch, give careful consideration to the type of permanent fixtures you introduce, as well as its layout, because you will want it to look good for a long time. Although you can change the decorative finish, it's a far greater upheaval to change the main elements of this room.

To plan the bathroom layout, draw the room to scale on graph paper, including the position of doors, windows and other fixed features such as plumbing, piping and radiators. Also draw your chosen bathroom fixtures to scale on graph paper and cut these out to make mini-templates to move around on your room plan.

Try out as many layout options as the existing fixed features allow. Imagine how each option would work, taking into account the way the door opens, the position of any windows, and whether there's enough moving and standing space around each item. This is also the stage to plan out the positioning of any tiling and possibly tongue-and-groove panelling, which is great for hiding pipes.

Slightly raised floors are also useful for this purpose. Also consider whether any partitioning is needed to divide up the room and create a little more wall space.

When you finalize your design, leave it for a couple of days, then come back to it fresh to see if it still feels right and fits all of the criteria. You now have a basic layout around which to design your decorative scheme.

If you are restricted by the existing plumbing and your bathroom fixtures are in poor condition, or a dated, stale colour, consider installing an inexpensive simple white bathroom suite – it might not be your ultimate dream, but it will dramatically improve the look and feel of the room and the impact that any decorative work will have. However, if you are stuck with your original bathroom suite, rest assured that a tremendous amount can be achieved decoratively. Vast improvements can be made with only a little imagination and flair, which this book aims to inspire and provide.

◄ The bath is given prime position in this bathroom with the sink and toilet fitted neatly and discreetly into the wall behind.

▼ Draw a scaled plan of the shape and fixed features of your bathroom. Cut out your bathroom fixtures, drawn at the same scale, and try out different layout options to fit with the room shape and fixed features.

Choosing surfaces and techniques

As bathrooms are functional rooms, choose a decorative technique that will not only fit the style of your bathroom, but will also be practical for the amount of usage and the level of ventilation the room will receive. As bathrooms are subject to condensation and changing temperatures, good ventilation is essential. Large family bathrooms need to stand up to the robust wear and tear that heavy traffic and frequent climatic changes produce, whereas guest bathrooms have a far lighter usage. Seal decorative schemes well to improve the longevity of the finish.

The bathroom provides many different surfaces to decorate, including walls, floors, bath panels, cabinets, frames, bathroom furniture, mirrors, curtains and shower curtains. You can plan a decorative scheme that will dramatically change the whole room or select specific areas to add extra quality and character.

Walls

Decorating the walls will have the most impact on the bathroom. Possibilities are far-reaching in terms of the techniques, styles and colours that can be used. Consider decorating a feature wall, or adding detail to a specific area, such as a faux mosaic splashback.

▲ Here relief shell stencils are applied to subtly contrasting, neutrally-coloured squares to make a stylish and elegant feature wall. See pages 72–75.

▲ Stencilled raised MDF squares stand out from plain panelling. See pages 60–63.

▶ Tongue-and-groove makes attractive furniture – here it is used as a New England-style cabinet, converted into a basin stand. See pages 84–87.

POSSIBILITIES INCLUDE:
- An overall colour theme using a monochromatic palette, with subtle tonal differences between walls, bath panel and woodwork; or a scheme using different colours on different walls.
- All-over stencilled pattern repeat, either as an occasional single repeated motif or a continuous block of pattern emulating the effect of wallpaper.
- Feature walls and panels.
- Hand painted or stencilled murals.
- Decorative detail to specific areas, such as splashbacks or decorative borders.
- Trompe L'Oeil and marble finishes to give a sense of luxury and calm.

Tongue-and-groove

Using tongue-and-groove panelling on bathroom walls is practical and has a timeless appeal. It gives both a feeling of calm and space – even in small areas – and a homely feel. Use it vertically or horizontally, covering part of the wall – up to dado height – or up to ceiling height to create a cool, lofty feeling. Associated with Swedish, New England and Shaker styles, it can be used to create both a modern or traditional setting.

Doors, woodwork and furniture

Painting doors, woodwork and furniture will accentuate them as specific features or as accents of colour and pattern to a main theme.

Floors

Painting floors is an inexpensive way to transform a room, often altering impressions of size and dimension. The best surfaces for painted floors are floorboards, hardboard or MDF (medium-density fibreboard). Providing the surface is well sealed and protected with floor varnish it should give sustained usage (see Varnishes and finishes for the bathroom, page 26). Bathrooms provide a well-defined, contained and manageable space to attempt a hand painted floor finish.

POSSIBILITIES INCLUDE:

- Pale washes for a bleached, whitewashed, weathered and cool finish.
- Transparent finishes emulating the rich, woody tones of inlay and marquetry.
- Solid opaque paint – New England style white floors.
- Simple chequerboard finish – Swedish style, squares or diamonds.
- Pattern repeats and borders.
- Faux mosaic using stencils.
- Stencilled tile designs.
- Marbled effects, in large tiles or slabs.

Tiles and glass

Speciality porcelain paints can be stencilled, sponged or hand painted on loose tiles and subsequently baked in a domestic oven before wall mounting. Glass accessories and ornaments can be decorated in the same way. Glass and mirrors can be given an etched finish using semi-permanent spray etching paint.

◀ This stencilled tile repeat perfectly emulates the look of thick ceramic floor tiles in bright polychromatic Mediterranean colours. See pages 108–111.

Fabrics

Stencilling and hand painting fabric can add a unique and beautiful touch to the bathroom. Fabrics can be made up into window curtains, blinds and shower curtains (hung with an inner waterproof shower curtain) as well as cushion or seat covers.

POSSIBILITIES INCLUDE:

- Single-motif stencil designs as a simple repeat.
- All-over repeat stencils.
- Hand painted stripes for a contemporary feel.

▲ Here porcelain paints are spattered onto tiles in a simple leaf design to make a clean, stylish splashback. See pages 64–67.

◀ Pastel coloured stripes of different widths are hand painted onto this sheer outer curtain to give a soft, yet crisp look. See pages 100–103.

Preparation

Preparation is a vital first step in decorating and plays an integral part in the quality of the finish. The bathroom, more than any other room in the house, is subject to dramatic changes in humidity and temperature levels, which have direct impact on decorated surfaces, and put an extra reliance on the quality of preparation to make the finish last. Proper preparation and careful basic decorating will mean that moisture will not get behind the paint and into the underlying plaster. Wood will be especially subject to expanding and contracting in these conditions, and therefore needs particular attention.

Allow plenty of time for preparation and priming and for base coat colours to dry thoroughly before any other finish is applied. This is known as 'curing' time and will mean that each successive surface treatment to be applied will adhere fully to the surface and have a longer life. The more time left between coats, the stronger and more durable the surface will be.

Dampness and moisture

As bathrooms are subject to condensation and changing temperatures, good ventilation is essential. If there are specific areas of dampness, these may have been caused either by lack of ventilation in a moisture-ridden atmosphere or by external problems. Residual dampness from external sources cannot be dealt with where it appears, as this will only cause the dampness to reappear elsewhere. The problem needs to be dealt with at its source, so it is important to seek professional advice. When the problem has been dealt with, treat the affected interior area with fungicide to kill mould spores (following the manufacturer's instructions).

PREPARATION OF DIFFERENT SURFACES

The basic principles to adhere to in preparing any surface are:
- Ensure the surface is clean and free from grease, dirt, and dust.
- Remove loose or flaking finishes.
- Fill any holes, blemishes or cracks.
- Sand the surface to level out filler and to remove blemishes and bumps, and to create a key for the next stage.
- Wipe down the surface to remove dust.
- Size or seal as necessary.
- Prime or undercoat.
- Apply base coat.

The following charts show you how to tackle preparation for walls, woodwork, furniture and floors.

BASIC EQUIPMENT AND MATERIALS FOR PREPARATION

Equipment	Materials
Cleaning cloths	Lint-free cloths, rags, decorator's sponges
Cleaning fluids, solutions	Diluted detergent; sugar soap; methylated spirits; paint thinner
Abrasives	Sandpaper and wet-and-dry sandpaper in fine, medium and coarse grade according to level of sanding needed; flexible sanding block; steel wool; wire brush
Scrapers, strippers, knives	Broad-blade metal paint scraper; narrow-blade metal paint scraper; triangular shave hook; utility knife
Brushes	Natural bristle decorator's brushes; dusting brush
Sealing	PVA or size for plaster, knotting solution for wood
Filling	Interior filler for walls and plaster; fine wood filler or putty for wood; frame sealant for gaps between plaster and woodwork; putty knife
Protective clothing	Overalls; aprons; rubber gloves; cotton gloves; face mask; safety goggles; ear plugs
Dust sheets	Cotton dust sheets, plastic sheeting, masking tape to tape down cloths

PREPARING WALLS

Wall surfaces	Method of preparation and materials
Newly plastered walls	Ceramic tiles can be applied to dry fresh plaster, but primer, emulsion, or wallpaper should not be applied for six months to allow plaster to dry out fully. Paint and decorative work applied too soon to new plaster will be subject to cracking. Traditional limewash may be applied, as it allows the plaster beneath to breathe. After appropriate drying, brush off dust or mineral salts and apply size or PVA, diluted according to manufacturer's instructions. Leave to dry out completely, then apply a coat of acrylic primer.
Newly skimmed plastered walls	Walls that have had a new coat of skimmed plaster need to be left to dry for 2–3 days, or until fully dry, before sizing and undercoating with acrylic primer.
Old plasterwork	Old plaster may need some filling (see cracked plaster below), dusting or wiping down before sizing and priming. If the surface crumbles easily, apply a stabilizing solution before painting.
Cracked plaster or paintwork	Always repair and fill cracks before painting. Use a wallpaper scraper or blade to scrape out loose material from cracks or holes. Hairline cracks should be raked out to create a key for filler. Dampen areas to be filled with a decorator's brush and fill with appropriate filler according to manufacturer's instructions. Use a putty knife to press the filler into cracks or holes. When thoroughly dry, sand with fine wet-and-dry sandpaper. Wipe area with a damp cloth before priming.
Covered with new lining	If walls are papered with new lining paper, paint first with a thin coat of acrylic primer (50:50 water to paint), followed with a full-strength coat of primer.
Covered with old peeling paper, or paper unsuitable for painting	Paper that is old or peeling will not provide a suitable surface for painting. Do not attempt a 'quick-cover-up', because it will not last. Wet paper with large brush or sponge soaked in hot water and score with a utility knife. Allow paper to soak for 10–15 minutes and repeat process. Use a wide metal scraper to scrape off the paper, being careful not to damage underlying plaster. Repeat until all traces of paper are removed. Alternatively use a steam stripper (available from DIY hire shops). Finally wash thoroughly with a scouring sponge, hot water and detergent. Allow to dry. Any cracks or holes will need to be filled (follow filling instructions above). Sand filler and wipe down with a damp cloth, before priming with acrylic primer.
Covered with hessian or other textured paper or vinyl paper	Textured and vinyl papers consist of two layers. The outer layer of textured papers can usually be peeled and scraped off. Vinyl papers can usually be peeled off in whole strips. Start at the bottom, taking hold of both corners of the strip and pull away firmly, pulling upwards. Remove the backing paper using the same method as above. If the backing paper is in really good condition, this can be used as a lining paper for your decoration, but do ensure there are no loose edges or corners (sand back).

Plaster painted with matt emulsion

▲ Sand rough or bumpy areas ▲ Prime over dark colours with white acrylic primer

If the surface is sound, remove any dirt and grease with sugar soap, and sand any rough or bumpy areas. Fill and sand any holes and cracks. Ensure area is free of dust. If you are covering a dark colour with a paler colour (e.g. pale yellow over blue or green, or white over red), prime the area first with white acrylic primer to ensure top colour stays 'true' and to assist good coverage.

Wall surfaces	Method of preparation and materials
Plaster painted with oil-based or acrylic gloss paint	Gloss paint that is to be covered with water-based paints needs particular attention, as water-based paint will not properly bond to shiny, non-absorbent surfaces. Remove dirt and grease with sugar soap, fill and sand any holes and cracks and sand the whole area thoroughly with medium-grade wet-and-dry sandpaper to create a key for painting. Wipe down with a damp cloth to remove dust and prime with an even coat of acrylic primer.
Lining paper previously painted with matt emulsion paint	If the surface is sound, remove any dirt and grease with sugar soap, and sand any rough or bumpy areas. Follow instructions above.
Lining paper previously painted with oil-based or acrylic gloss paint	Providing the surface is sound, treat as a plaster wall painted with same treatment. Follow instructions above.

New tongue-and-groove (T&G)

▲ Apply knotting solution

Sand down wood and apply knotting solution to knots and resinous patches, to prevent discolouration to subsequent treatments. Fill any holes in the wood with fine wood filler and sand to a smooth finish, in the direction of the grain. Wipe off dust and apply two coats of acrylic primer, working it well into the joints.

Wall surfaces	Method of preparation and materials
Painted T&G previously painted with water-based, acrylic paint	Clean and sand with medium-grade wet-and-dry sandpaper. Fill any holes with fine wood filler and sand to a smooth finish. Remove dust and apply a good coat of acrylic primer. Strip thick and bumpy paint with an appropriate paint stripper. Sand and then apply an even coat of acrylic primer.

Continued over page ☛

PREPARING WALLS

Wall surfaces	Method of preparation and materials
Painted T&G previously painted with oil-based paints	Clean and sand the whole area thoroughly with medium-grade wet-and-dry paper. Wash down. For uneven, flaking or blistered paintwork, scrape off or strip with an appropriate paint stripper. Sand down and fill any holes with wood filler. Sand and then apply an even coat of acrylic primer.
Bare, new MDF	Sand with fine-grade wet-and-dry sandpaper to a smooth finish. Apply one coat watered down PVA (1 part PVA to 3 parts water). Follow with one coat acrylic primer. Make sure all cut edges of timber are sealed as well. Apply two coats of chosen base colour.
Preparing a wall for tiling	Plaster in good condition is the ideal surface for tiling. Irregular plaster should be re-skimmed before applying tiles. A wall already tiled also offers a good surface, provided the tiles are firmly stuck to the wall and not chipped or broken. Use standard tile adhesive, but take care to stagger the new tiles, so that the joins do not line up with those underneath. Walls previously painted with gloss or emulsion paint are not suitable surfaces for tiling, as the tile adhesive needs to stick directly to the wall not to paint. Use coarse sandpaper to roughen the wall before tiling. Tiling should not be attempted onto any papered surface, as the tiles will only stick to the paper, which will not be strong enough to hold the tiles. Strip the paper from the walls before starting to tile.

▲ Apply tile adhesive to wall.

▲ Position tiles using tile spacers between tiles.

▲ Fill gaps with grout adhesive, removing excess with damp cloth.

PREPARING DOORS, WOODWORK AND CABINETS

Doors, cabinets, furniture, woodwork	Preparation for washes or effects where wood shows through	Preparation for painted and decorative finishes
To prepare new, bare wood	Fill any cracks, holes or blemishes with fine wood filler. Sand with fine-grade or wet-and-dry sandpaper in the direction of the grain of the wood until smooth. Apply knotting solution to knots to prevent discolouration from wood resin.	Fill any cracks, holes or blemishes with fine wood filler. Sand with fine-grade or wet-and-dry sandpaper in the direction of the grain of the wood until smooth. Apply knotting solution to knots. Apply one coat of acrylic primer and two coats of base-paint colour, taking care to paint the ends of cut timber.
To prepare wood painted with water-based or acrylic paints	Strip paint with appropriate paint stripper following the manufacturer's instructions. Wash off remains of stripper. If the paint is not too thick it may be possible to remove it using medium-grade or wet-and-dry sandpaper. Fill any holes or cracks with fine wood filler and sand the whole area with fine-grade or wet-and-dry sandpaper, following the direction of the grain.	Clean and fill any holes or cracks with fine wood filler. Sand down and prime with acrylic primer. If woodwork is covered with thick, bumpy layers of paint, strip back to wood with paint stripper. Sand and prime after stripping. Apply two coats of chosen base-paint colour.
To prepare wood painted with oil-based paints	Follow instructions for stripping and preparing wood painted with water-based paints. You may however need several applications of paint stripper.	Wash down and sand thoroughly to create a key, then prime with acrylic primer. If original paint is uneven, flaking or blistered, scrape off or strip. Fill any cracks with fine wood filler. Sand and prime with acrylic primer.
To prepare wood previously coated with water-based varnish	Wash with diluted detergent, fill any holes or cracks with fine wood filler and sand with fine-grade or wet-and-dry sandpaper.	Wash with diluted detergent; fill any holes or cracks with fine wood filler and sand with fine-grade sandpaper or wet-and-dry sandpaper. Apply one coat of acrylic primer and two coats of chosen base colour.
To prepare wood previously coated with oil-based varnish	Strip varnish with appropriate paint stripper following the manufacturer's instructions. Wash off remains of stripper. If the varnish is not too thick it may be possible to remove it using medium-grade or wet-and-dry sandpaper. Fill any holes or cracks with fine wood filler and sand whole area with fine-grade or wet-and-dry sandpaper, following direction of the grain.	Wash down and sand thoroughly to create a key, then prime with acrylic primer. If original varnish is uneven, flaking or blistered, scrape off or strip. Fill any cracks with fine wood filler. Sand and prime with acrylic primer, followed by two coats of chosen base colour.
Bare, new medium-density fibreboard	Not applicable	Sand with fine-grade or wet-and-dry sandpaper to a smooth finish. Apply one coat watered down PVA (1 part white (PVA) glue to 3 parts water). Follow with one coat acrylic primer. Make sure all cut edges of board are sealed as well. Apply two coats of chosen base colour.

PREPARING FLOORS FOR PAINTING

Floor surfaces	*Method of preparation*
New floorboards for washes or stains	New boards that have not been stained and are clean should not need sanding. Scrub down with hot water and detergent to remove surface dirt and any dirt around nail holes. Leave to dry thoroughly. The floor is now ready for washes, stains and varnishes. Apply wood bleach to decrease the yellowing effect of pine.
New floorboards for painted or decorative finishes	Follow instructions above. When the floor is clean and dry apply two coats of acrylic primer. The primer will allow the top coat to go on smoothly, to cover well and give a longer life.
Old floorboards for washes or stains	A floor sander will remove the previous layers of paint and varnish (see Sanding Floors). However, if the floorboards have a dark stain on them, consider the amount of preparation involved carefully before deciding on a transparent finish. Dark wood stain will have seeped right into the fabric of the wood and will prove very difficult to remove, even with deep sanding. Floorboards like this are best sanded and painted. Test a small area by sanding and rubbing back with steel wool and methylated spirits: if the stain lifts, then it may be worth the effort of sanding the whole floor.
Old floorboards for painted or decorative finishes	Follow the instructions for Sanding Floors. Once the surface is smooth, clean and free from dust, prime with two coats of acrylic primer before applying your chosen base coat.
MDF (medium-density fibreboard) for painted or decorative finishes	MDF and hardboard can be laid directly onto existing floorboards. Ensure floorboards are flat and secure, with no protruding nails. Use boards that are 4' (122 cm) square, 3' (90 cm) square, or 4' × 2' (122 × 60 cm). Refer to a comprehensive DIY manual or get a professional to lay the boards (hardboard should be laid shiny side up). Hardboard must be conditioned (moistened) before laying, and MDF must be sealed with PVA glue once laid. Prime either surface with two coats of acrylic primer before applying your chosen base coat.

FLAT PAINTING WALLS

The quality of decorative finishes is largely dependent on the surface they are applied to. A well-painted wall provides this surface. Use a paintbrush wherever possible, as this will give a smooth surface – a roller leaves a bumpy surface, unsuitable for stencilling or marbling. Follow these simple steps for correct flat painting, after priming.

◀ *Use as wide a brush as you can manage comfortably. Working in sections across the wall, apply a generous amount of paint to the wall, and spread across the area in large criss-cross strokes, until the paint is evenly distributed. This process is known as 'laying on'.*

◀ *Then brush upwards and downwards through the paint in long, vertical strokes, creating as smooth a surface as possible. This process is known as 'laying off'.*

SANDING FLOORS

Equipment	Electric floor sander; edging sander (from DIY hire shops); sanding belts (in coarse, medium and fine grade); nail punch and claw hammer; steel wool; methylated spirits.
Protection	Protective clothing; rubber and cotton gloves; face mask, and you may also want to wear goggles, to protect eyes from dust, and ear plugs, to block out the noise of the sander.
Making good	Punch all nails into floor to prevent tearing the sander. Remove old carpet tacks etc.
Removing wax	Some floors may have previous coats or patches of wax or polish. Remove with steel wool and methylated spirits to avoid clogging up the sander. Wear protective gloves.
Seal room	Seal off room completely, using plastic sheeting and masking tape to cover doors and windows. Sanding is a very dusty process, dust will get into every nook and cranny of the house if not prevented. Where possible, leave a window open for ventilation.
Sanding main floor	Start near the edges of the room (slightly away from the wall to avoid damaging the boards). For a room needing heavy sanding, work the sander in diagonal lines across the room and then run it down the length of the floorboards. Never sand straight across the floorboards as this will gouge and damage the floor. For a room needing only light sanding work along the length of the boards, always lift the belt at the end of each run to avoid damaging the board. Do not allow the belt to sit stationary on the floor while on, as this also will gouge the floor.
Sanding edges	Use an edging sander to sand up to the boards, taking care not to damage them in the process.
Cleaning up	It is advisable to vacuum at regular intervals during sanding (some sanding machines have a dust bag attached) and very thoroughly after sanding is complete. Allow the dust in the room to settle for a couple of hours, and then vacuum again. Finally, use a lint-free, dry cloth to remove all remaining dust. It is better not to wet the floor at this stage, as water may mark the wood. The floor is now ready for your chosen finish.

Paints

All paint comprises a pigment, a binder and a medium. Pigment provides colour and covering power; the binder provides adhesion to the surface; and the medium makes application possible. The terms water-based and oil-based refer to the binder and medium and indicate which solvent is needed for thinning and cleaning. These are the two main and most widely used paint types. Wherever possible, water-based paints are used throughout this book, as they are far safer, more environmentally friendly, easy to use, and won't discolour over time.

Paints to use in the bathroom

Glossy emulsion is non-absorbent and matt emulsion is absorbent. Decorative techniques, such as stencilling, stamping and hand painting, are best applied to matt emulsion painted surfaces sealed with a coat of acrylic matt varnish. This gives a matt surface that allows the decoration to adhere and bond to the surface and will allow you to wipe off any marks without damaging or discolouring the painted surface. Shiny paints will cause the stencilling or stamping to glance off the surface, and to smudge, bleed and fail to adhere properly. Once the decoration is complete a final coat of acrylic matt varnish can be added for extra protection.

Marbling and other techniques involving scumble glaze can be applied to semi-gloss or satin emulsion surfaces, but the paint must be applied very carefully to avoid ridges and brush strokes showing. Matt emulsion with acrylic matt varnish is an ideal surface for these techniques.

For general flat painting or painting wooden tongue-and-groove surfaces choose either matt emulsion, or wood paint with acrylic matt varnish for a more chalky finish or vinyl silk, mid-sheen emulsions, or acrylic eggshell for a slightly shiny surface.

The following charts give a brief description of the main primers, paints and specialty paints which are used in this book (see Resource Directory, page 124, for suppliers).

PRIMERS, SEALANTS AND TREATMENTS

Type	Description	Uses	Coverage per litre
Wood bleach	Caustic bleach solution for lightening wood.	Effective in eliminating yellow effect of pine. Used for treating floorboards.	As per manufacturer's guidelines.
Knotting solution	A shellac-based sealing solution to prevent seepage from resinous areas.	Specifically for knots or resinous patches on new, untreated wood.	As per manufacturer's guidelines, but a little goes a long way.
Acrylic primer	A water-based primer, which seals surfaces and forms a key for other paints to adhere to.	Priming new or exposed wood, hardboard, MDF, new plaster, lining paper and as an undercoat for emulsion. For use on walls, ceilings, floors and woodwork.	Up to 12 sq m (13 sq yd).

Coverage

When buying paint, be generous with your calculations and buy slightly more than you think you need. Never underestimate. Paint is made in batches, and colours may vary slightly from batch to batch.

HEALTH, SAFETY AND ENVIRONMENTAL CONSIDERATIONS

• Keep all decorating materials and products out of the reach of children.

When working with paints and paint products:

• Always read and follow the manufacturer's instructions for all products.
• Always work in a well-ventilated area.
• Avoid allowing paint or paint products to come into contact with the skin and eyes.
• Wear protective gloves when working with oil-based and methylated spirit-based products.
• Wear protective gloves, mask and goggles when sanding, using chemical strippers, spray paints, glues or metallic powders.
• Wherever possible use products that are safe for the environment.
• Do not empty paints and solvents into drains or water systems.
• Where possible, take waste paint to the nearest household disposal site.

PAINTS FOR WALLS, CEILINGS, FLOORS AND WOOD

Type	Description	Uses	Coverage per litre
Emulsion – matt or semi-gloss	Water plus latex-based paint. Higher quality matt versions contain more pigment and chalk, giving a less plastic look.	Painting walls and ceiling, can also be used on floors and furniture. Semi-gloss version not suitable as base for stencilling or stamping.	Up to 10–13 sq m (11–14 sq yd), depending on brand.
Bathroom and kitchen emulsion	Water plus latex-based paint designed for moist conditions. Mid-sheen finish, wipeable, hardwearing, but gives a plastic look.	Painting walls and ceiling, can also be used on floors and furniture – not suitable as a base for stencilling or stamping.	Up to 10–13 sq m (11–14 sq yd), depending on brand.
Metallic emulsion	Water-based latex paint for an all-over metallic finish. Durable, wipeable finish.	Painting walls and can also be used on furniture and for decorative finishes.	Up to 10–13 sq m (11–14 sq yd), depending on brand.
Impasto, plaster paint or 3-D modelling paint	Water-based, thick paint for creating textured surfaces or relief stencils. (Can be homemade by adding powdered chalk to emulsion for textured finishes.)	Painting walls and as a decorative finish on wood or medium-density fibreboard. Can be coloured with universal tinters, or colourwashed over.	Up to 4 sq m (4 sq yd).
Wood paint	A matt, opaque, water-based paint with built-in primer. High chalk and pigment content. Covers well. Better quality than emulsion. Should be sealed and protected with acrylic varnish.	Specially formulated for wood, furniture and floors. Use full-strength for flat painting, distressing and stencilling, or diluted for washes.	Up to 12 sq m (13 sq yd) undiluted.
Acrylic eggshell	Water-based eggshell paint with a satin sheen finish. Replacement for oil-based versions. Low odour and does not discolour over time.	Painting woodwork and furniture and as a base to scumble-glaze effects.	Up to 12 sq m (13 sq yd).
Oil-based eggshell	Oil-based eggshell paint with a satin sheen finish. High odour, will discolour with oxidization, but does flow well when applying.	Painting woodwork and furniture.	Up to 14 sq m (15 sq yd).
Oil-based gloss paint	Oil-based gloss paint with a gloss shine finish. High odour, will discolour with oxidization, but does flow well when applying.	Painting woodwork.	Up to 14 sq m (15 sq yd).

SPECIALITY AND DECORATIVE PAINTS AND MEDIUMS

Type	Description	Uses	Coverage per litre
Stencil and stamp paint	Water-based decorative paint generally flows better than emulsions. Available in matt, metallic and glitter colours.	Suitable for use on matt emulsion, wood paint, colourwash, or impasto (relief) surfaces. Some brands also suitable for fabrics.	As per manufacturer's guidelines.
Tile paint	A water-based paint, which gives a semi-water-resistant finish.	Painting ceramic tiles in areas not subject to direct contact with water.	Up to 10 sq m (11 sq yd).
Porcelain and earthenware paint	Water-based decorative paint, suitable for baking for a durable, water-resistant finish.	Decorating ceramic, porcelain and earthenware surfaces. Good for decorating tiles before wall mounting.	45 ml (3 tbsp) will cover up to ten 10 cm sq (4") tiles when painted as solid colour.
Glass frosting/ etching spray	Solvent-based spray medium, semi-water-resistant finish.	Suitable for glass, windows, mirrors, but not for wet conditions.	Varies by application.
Acrylic scumble glaze	Water-based acrylic transparent, colourless glaze. Should be sealed and protected with acrylic varnish.	Used to create a wide range of paint effects. Also used for wood-graining and marbling effects. Dries to a satin finish.	Up to 16 sq m (17 sq yd), varies according to dilution.
Colourwash	Transparent, water-based glaze. Available either coloured or clear for tinting. Should be sealed with acrylic varnish.	Designed for use on walls, also good for translucent stencilling.	Up to 30 sq m (33 sq yd).
Universal tinters	Concentrated, water-based tinting agent in liquid form. Disperses well.	Used to tint acrylic scumble glaze, clear colourwash, acrylic varnishes, thick textured paints and 3-D stencil paste.	2–3 drops will adequately colour 1 liter (2 pt) of scumble, clear colourwash or acrylic varnish.
Gilding size	Water-based glue of milky consistency.	Applying Dutch metal, metal leaf and metallic powders.	As per manufacturer's guidelines.

Equipment and tools for the job

Before starting any decorative project, gather all of the equipment you will need to complete the job successfully, so that everything is easily close at hand. The charts below show the basic equipment you will need for the projects in this book.

DRAWING AND MARKING EQUIPMENT

Equipment	Uses
Spirit level	Vital aid to creating vertical and horizontal registration guides on walls
Set square	Angles, north and south axes on floors and walls
Tape measures 30 cm and 45 cm (12" and 18")	Larger wall and floor measurements
Plastic rulers	Measuring, registering and marking up
Chalk reel	String in container of chalk for making registration guidelines
Masking tape; low-tack masking tape; painting tape	Masking off areas
Lining tape in 5 mm and 1 cm (¼" and ½") widths	Masking tile and pattern repeats and for edging decoration
HB pencil	Drawing and marking (a hard pencil makes light marks, but press lightly)
Plastic rubber	Removing pencil marks

BRUSHES AND GENERAL EQUIPMENT

Brush/equipment	Uses
Low-tack masking tape	Masking off light switches, plug sockets, etc. when painting
5–10 cm (2–4") decorator's brushes – natural bristle	Priming and painting emulsions, eggshells, gloss paints, and general usage
5–10 cm (2–4") decorator's brushes – synthetic bristle	Priming, painting and varnishing emulsions, acrylic eggshell, and acrylic varnishes
5–10 cm (2–4") varnish brushes	Applying shellacs and varnishes
Fitches	Mixing paints, for edges, moldings, and cutting in
Artist's sable brushes	Hand painting and detail, also application of gilding size to small areas
5 mm and 1 cm (¼" and ½") one-stroke brushes in sable or nylon	Hand painting, good for creating clean edges. Nylon versions are good for painting on tiles
Stencil brushes	For stippling and fine spattering
Hog-hair softener	Softening, blending acrylic glaze effects (e.g. marbling), colourwash effects
Badger softener	Fine softening in glaze work
Stippling block	Stippling glazes as grainy, veil-of-colour or textured effects in thick paint
Natural sea sponge	Sponging broken glaze effects
Decorator's steel float	Applying thick plaster paint (can also use a large palette knife)
Paint kettle	Mixing paint glazes and emulsions
Surgical gloves	Useful for glaze work, such as sponging
Tack cloth	Impregnated cloth for removing dust and particles, excellent for wiping down decorated surfaces before varnishing

Care of brushes

It is worth investing in good equipment and brushes. Quality brushes will improve with wear, as the tips of the bristles will become rounded, whereas the bristles in cheaper brushes tend to be poorly secured and will fall out during use. Your brushes will have a long life if they are well cared for. Avoid soaking for long periods, as this loosens the glue that holds the bristles in place. Wash promptly after use, to avoid paint caking in the bristles. Never let acrylic scumble glazes dry out on brushes, as the tips will be ruined for fine or soft work, and will be difficult to restore.

1 Remove excess paint with water, apply a little detergent to the bristles, and use a nailbrush to brush through the bristles and remove all traces of paint.

2 Rinse and dip in diluted fabric conditioner or hair conditioner to keep the bristles soft and in good condition.

3 Rinse and squeeze out, shake out excess water and leave to dry flat initially, and then hang, if possible, with the bristles pointing down.

STENCILLING AND STAMPING EQUIPMENT

Equipment	Uses
Photocopy, layout, sketch paper	Sketches, designs and layouts
Pencils, black felt-tip pen	Drawing designs
Black permanent marker	Marking registration guides on Mylar
Sticky tape and scissors	Sticking paper design to Mylar, cutting paper designs etc.
Mylar	Clear plastic sheets for cutting stencils
Scalpel or craft knife	Cutting stencil designs
Metal ruler	Cutting straight lines in stencils
Self-healing cutting mat	Surface for cutting stencils
Repositionable spray adhesive	Securing stencils to all surfaces, prevents bleeding
Masking tape; low-tack masking tape, and painting tape	Masking-off around stencil, protecting edges
Paper plate or palette	Stencil and stamp paints (extra one for inking up stamp roller)
High-density foam in 4 cm (1½") squares	Stencilling onto all surfaces, gives good application and control
Stencil brushes	Alternative for stencilling, though not as controlled
Paper towel	Dabbing off excess paint from stencil sponges
Mini-roller	Inking-up stamp
Ready-made stamp	Stamping motifs
Pre-cut stencil	Stencilling designs

Stencilling techniques

Stencilling is an extremely versatile way to add pattern to a host of decorative schemes. Templates for all the stencils featured in the projects in this book can be found on pages 114–123. The stencils can also be purchased pre-cut from the author's web-site – www.hennydonovanmotif.co.uk.

Single motif design

Stencil design is based on the idea of cutting away shapes to create a positive pattern. This is done by creating a series of interlinking bridges between the cut-out shapes that hold the design together. Although stencilling can be very intricate, the process involved is really not complex and it is possible to create your own stencil design with a minimum of drawing skills.

◀ A reverse stencil can also be created, which is where the cut-out shape is used to stencil a negative image – this is ideal for etching.

3 SECURING STENCIL

Lightly draw some guide marks in pencil or chalk onto the wall to position the stencil. Use a ruler and spirit level to ensure vertical and horizontal accuracy. Spray repositionable glue onto the back of the stencil and secure to the wall.

4 STENCILLING YOUR DESIGN

To achieve good quality results stencil with a piece of high-density sponge. Pull the corners of the sponge together, dip into the stencil paint, and then dab off the excess on some kitchen towel. It is very important not to overload the sponge as too much paint will smear over the template and is likely to bleed beneath the design. Apply in light sweeping movements over the stencil.

1 DRAWING YOUR MOTIF

Find a photograph or line drawing of an image you want to recreate. Trace over the main elements of the picture. Lay another piece of tracing paper or layout paper over your first tracing and start to separate the main shapes, incorporating the 'bridges' between the shapes to be cut out. Work in pencil, and be prepared for a bit of trial and error.

2 CUTTING YOUR DESIGN

Photocopy your finished design and stick it onto the back of a piece of Mylar – a transparent film designed for stencils. Lay the design onto a self-healing cutting mat and use a sharp scalpel or craft knife to carefully cut away the main shapes of your design (or cut around your design if you are creating a reverse stencil). Use an even pressure to cut through the Mylar and take care not to cut through the bridges you have created in your design. It will take a little practice to cut out accurately the shapes you have drawn. Some shapes, such as circles and flowers, can be harder to cut, but designs with squares and rectangles, such as mosaic, are much easier to cut to start with.

◀ A design may have more than one layer, where extra detail is added on top of the first shapes that you create. These should be drawn within the first-layer shapes to ensure future registration, as shown in the design above. Registration dots can also be made in the corners, so that the two layers will line up – use a pencil to make registration marks when printing.

Repeat design

There are many types of repeat design. These include:

A Single motifs simply repeated in rows or columns, or in squares or diamond patterns.

B Border repeats where the design has a continuous linear repeat.

C All-over repeats where the design is adapted to flow continuously across the surface with no obvious joins – great for creating realistic wallpaper effects. This is done by simply inverting the design and adapting it.

Designing a continuous repeat stencil

Try out several designs and experiment with photocopying your design to see how the repeat works before you print. Designs with flowers and leaves adapt easily into repeat patterns.

1 Draw out your chosen design and trim the sides of the paper. Draw a vertical line down the middle of the design at points where there are or could be natural breaks. Label the left and right edges A and B. Cut carefully along this line.

2 Turn the two halves over and stick back to back, so that the left and right edges are now in the middle, as are the A and B. There will be an empty space left in the middle. Add extra motifs into this space to create a feeling of continuity. You may also need to rub out some elements of the original drawing to make it work.

3 Now draw a horizontal line through the middle of the design and label the two outer edges C and D.

4 Cut carefully along this line and stick the two halves back to back, lining up the two joins to make a perfect cross in the middle of the design. If the middle is not lined up in a cross, the design will not repeat correctly. A 'step' may appear at either edge – this is a natural part of the design, so don't be tempted to try to make the edges line up. Add extra motifs to the centre of the design, rubbing out any elements of the original drawing that no longer fit.

Positioning repeat designs

If you are applying a repeat stencil as a wallpaper style repeat you will have to deal with corners and creating straight vertical drops.

▶ Use a ruler, set square and permanent marker to draw two lines across the top and down the left-hand side of the Mylar. Use a level to make horizontal and vertical marks across the top and down the left-hand side of the wall.

Position the first repeat in the left-hand corner of the wall by matching the lines on the Mylar against the marks on the wall. The second repeat should then be directly under the first. Make vertical registration marks for the second drop and position stencil as for the first. Repeat this across the wall using the level to check that the design is straight.

5 Photocopy the new design three times, cut out the design, and stick them together to check that they all line up for the repeat. It may take several attempts to get a design to work well, and in the early stages you may want to work with an outline drawing, getting it to repeat correctly and then adapting to a stencil design with bridges. With practice you will be able to draw out the design in the stencil format.

6 Make small registration dots in the corner of the design, if it is a two-layer design. Cut out following cutting instructions, step 2, Single motif design.

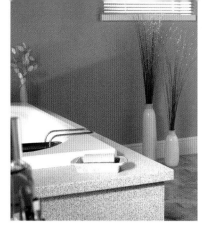

COLOUR

Colour is the most powerful and inspirational tool you have when decorating. Throughout history, we have always made use of colour in our homes; from the earthy pigments in early cave dwellings, to 21st-century paints available in literally any colour.

The colour of a room will affect you every time you walk into it, as colour can alter the mood and atmosphere, making it invigorating or energizing; restful or healing; and so forth. The spectrum of colours available creates a spectrum of possible moods and feelings. This is why colour choices are largely subjective, motivated by what you like, and what makes you feel good. Some people will feel invigorated by green, but for others, it might be blue or pink.

Colour will be integral to your design decisions for the bathroom, right down to the colour of the bathroom suite, even if it is just plain white. Your starting point might be a favourite colour, or it might be a bathroom accessory that you could build a theme around. Conversely, you might be attracted to a decorating style that looks best in a particular colour, or you may have a bathroom suite in a singularly uninspiring colour that needs 'knocking back' in the colour scheme.

There is a huge range of possibilities available, which can sometimes make choosing colour schemes a little baffling. Give yourself time to choose your colour scheme: test the colours by painting samples onto large sheets of paper and hanging them up so that you can see how you react to them over the course of a few days.

Cool and warm colours

All colour schemes derive from the basic relationships between colours. The colour wheel is a helpful tool in understanding this relationship. It shows how the three primary colours (red, yellow and blue) relate to the three secondary colours (orange, green and violet) and the tertiary colours (where a primary is mixed with an adjacent secondary). Distinct cooler and warmer sides of the colour spectrum can be seen, as well as the strengths of the different colour intensities and tonal values.

Using warm and cool colours can create different moods. Cooler colours are known for their receding effect, making spaces feel larger and more airy. Warmer colours have the effect of advancing, and will appear to fill a space more. They are energizing and active and also give a closed-in feeling, which can be cosy and contained.

Blue · **Green** · Violet · **Yellow** · **Red** · Orange

▲ Colour wheel

▲ Warm colours   ▲ Cool colours

Each colour itself also has a cool and warm side. For example, there are warm, mossy greens and cooler sea greens; or cooler pale lemon and warm, sunny yellow. This can be used to great effect in altering the dynamics and atmosphere of a room.

Our association with the bathroom is that it should be a place to relax. For this reason cool colours are perennial favorites for bathrooms. However, brighter, more active colours – reds, yellows and oranges – could be good choices for busy family bathrooms, to move the clientele on and out!

▲ Cool green   ▲ Warm green

Colour and light

Light has a dramatic effect on colour, so the quality of a colour will depend on the quality of the light illuminating it. Daylight will create natural shadows and highlights, bringing out the different tones of a colour, while artificial light has the effect of flattening out colours. Normally, it is best to choose colour in daylight, but if your bathroom has no windows, colour-check in the room itself.

Colour also has a definite effect on light, as different colours will reflect or absorb light at different rates. Lighter colours reflect light, causing the colour to appear further away than it really is. Darker colours absorb light and so the colour appears closer than it really is. It is useful to consider the size of the room, the source of light and the effects of these on the colour you are considering.

Colours that work together

The projects and variations in this book have been chosen to demonstrate how different colour schemes work in the bathroom. Most colour schemes are based on either synchronizing colours, or colours that work by their contrasting elements which are utilized to the full.

MONOCHROMATIC, TONAL PALETTES

Tone-on-tone, restricted monochromatic palettes make use of the different tones and intensities of a single colour and create a unified scheme. A truly monochromatic palette will stay within either the warm or cool grades of a colour. For example, purple or mauve moving towards the cooler, blue side of the spectrum, gives tones from pale lavender to deeper violet; whereas purple, on the warmer, red side of the spectrum gives more pinky tones of pale lilac through to rich purple. Green at the warmer end gives pale limes and moss colours (see Modern Swedish style, page 60), but at the cool end produces pale mint and aqua shades.

The monochromatic palette comprises a range of tones derived from an original colour: light tones, known as tints (where white is added), and darker tones, known as shades (where black is added). The easiest way to use a monochromatic palette is to take a mid-tone colour (such as green) and add successive amounts of white or ivory to

obtain the paler tints. Mix three or four tones in total.

Monochromatic schemes in neutral colours also work well using tones of off-white, stone, taupe (cool), or ivory, pale sand and honey-beige (warm). Start with the lightest colour, and tint to the required shade using differing amounts of raw umber, burnt sienna and yellow ochre.

POLYCHROMATIC, COLOURFUL PALETTES

Polychromatic schemes make use of different colours that share the same tonal value and intensity. A selection of colours with the same strength can have a natural colour affinity, even if they are quite diverse. Modern brightly coloured schemes make good use of this kind of palette (see Colour Combos, pages 98–113), which is a contemporary take on more traditional schemes.

You can choose these colours by using small paint cards. Line up the corresponding level on each chart to see how the colours work together.

HARMONIOUS COLOUR SCHEMES

Harmonious colours lie next to each other on the colour wheel, so blend together decoratively. They work successfully using varying tonal strengths, so pale and stronger colours can be used here.

CONTRASTING COLOUR SCHEMES

Contrasting schemes can be based on colours that have a stark contrast, such as black, or charcoal, and white, as seen in chequerboard tiles or striking marbles (see Calacatta marble, page 92), ultramarine and white, or colours based on more subtle contrasts, such as patterns in chambray blue and off-white (see Toile du Jouy variation, page 49).

COMPLEMENTARY COLOUR SCHEMES

Colours that lie opposite each other on the colour wheel are known as 'complementary' or 'opposite' colours. Schemes that use complementary colours work by using these contrasts. Complementary colour schemes often need only a dash of one colour against a backdrop of the other. These contrasts don't have to be painted; they can be added with accessories, flowers or plants.

METALLICS With their ability to complement any colour, metallics can appear quite neutral or act as a strong contrast. This is partly because of their reflective surface and partly because they have neutral colours beneath their lustre. Silver is probably the most versatile metallic colour, working with a multitude of different schemes.

▲ Polychromatic palette

▲ Harmonious palette

▲ Contrasting palette

▲ Complementary palette

▲ Metallics

▲ Monochromatic tones of purple

FINISHING & STYLING

Sealing

It is essential to seal and protect decorative finishes in the bathroom carefully, to make your work last and to keep it looking good. Sealing will make the finishes moisture resistant so that they will withstand the heavy wear and tear of the bathroom environment, including the regular wiping down of surfaces and frequent humid conditions.

This is particularly important in a bathroom that is used intensely, such as a busy family bathroom, as moisture can gradually work its way behind the paintwork and into the underlying plaster. In cases like this, apply an extra coat of acrylic varnish, and allow plenty of drying time between coats so that each coat has time to adhere fully to the wall before the next coat is applied. Also, ensure the room is well ventilated to disperse the humidity.

If the bathroom is used less, such as a guest bathroom with infrequent traffic, you may need only one coat of varnish. This is especially applicable if the room is well-ventilated.

VARNISHES AND FINISHES FOR THE BATHROOM

Type	Description	Uses	Coverage per quart
Metallic or pearlescent varnish	Water-based varnish with pearly, metallic lustre. Gives medium protection.	For adding metallic lustre to painted or bare wood surfaces. More suited for lighter colours, as darker colours can be difficult to cover smoothly.	Up to 16 sq m (17 sq yd).
Acrylic varnish	Water-based varnish available in matt (also known as dead flat), eggshell (also known as satin or semi-matt), or gloss finishes. Quick drying.	To seal and protect all water-based painted surfaces on walls, floors, woodwork and furniture.	Up to 16 sq m (17 sq yd).
Acrylic floor varnish, also known as water-based polyurethane	Tough acrylic varnish specially formulated for floors.	Suitable for use over bare and painted floors.	As per manufacturer's guide-lines.
Cellulose-resin-based varnish	An extremely tough two-part lacquer, with a resin catalyst.	For rooms receiving extra-heavy foot traffic.	As per manufacturer's guide-lines.
Polyurethane varnish	Oil-based varnish in satin and gloss finishes. Adds a yellow luster to surface. Will yellow over time with oxidization. High odour.	For furniture, woodwork and floors.	Up to 14 sq m (15 sq yd).

Walls and wall finishes

If a flat coat of colour has originally been applied in bathroom paints, semi-gloss, or acrylic eggshell emulsion paints, varnishing is unnecessary. Walls painted in matt emulsion may, however, need a coat of water-based acrylic varnish for extra protection, although some matt emulsions do actually have a built-in sheen – test this by looking side on to see if the paint has a sheen, or alternatively wipe a small patch with a damp cloth to see how it reacts.

Use water-based acrylic varnishes on walls that have a decorative finish. Acrylic varnishes are strongly recommended for use in the projects throughout this book and are available in matt, eggshell and gloss levels of sheen (see chart).

Acrylic varnishes are easy to use and dry quickly. They also have no odour and are non-toxic. They give a strong, durable, water-resistant finish, and they will not yellow over time, which is

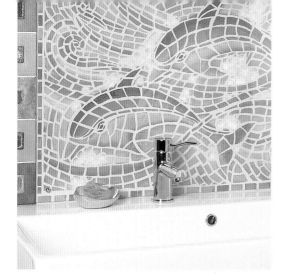

an important consideration for decorative finishes for which you have taken time and trouble in putting your colour scheme together. They also will not crack or chip in moist conditions in the way that an oil-based varnish will do in time.

Matt, eggshell and gloss types of acrylic varnish are perfect for walls; although the eggshell and gloss varieties are recommended for walls that are to be wiped down frequently, as they have a higher degree of durability. It is highly recommended that all decorative finishes are wiped over carefully with a tack cloth to remove all dust particles before varnishing.

Polyurethane varnishes are not recommended for walls at all, because of difficulty of application, patchy finish, yellowing and cracking over time.

Woodwork and furniture

Use acrylic eggshell and gloss to seal bare, unpainted woodwork and furniture. You can also tint the varnish if you want to 'antique' or tone down the wood or add a little colour to the finish. Alternatively use polyurethane varnish. Apply two coats of whichever varnish you choose.

Use acrylic eggshell or gloss varnish on woodwork or furniture that has a water-based decorative finish or an emulsion or wood paint finish. Do not use polyurethane varnish as this will discolour and spoil the appearance.

It is unnecessary to varnish woodwork or furniture painted with oil-based eggshell, satin or gloss (acrylic varnish will not adhere to oil-based surfaces).

Do not use polish or waxes on woodwork or furniture in the bathroom as they are not water-resistant and will mark every time they are splashed with water.

Floors

As well as using standard acrylic eggshell or gloss varnish on floors, you can use the special, tougher water-based floor varnishes that are now available, as shown in the chart.

The acrylic version of these is a tough, water-based polyurethane that can be applied either direct to bare wood or onto a decorated surface that has first been sealed with standard acrylic gloss varnish – this is to prevent any reaction between the painted surface and the water-based polyurethane varnish.

An even tougher option exists, which is a cellulose-resin-based varnish. The resin is added before application and acts as a catalyst to the cellulose base, creating a highly durable finish. Again it is advisable to seal painted finishes with a standard coat of acrylic gloss varnish to prevent any reaction between the painted surface and the cellulose varnish. Always read the manufacturer's instructions carefully before application.

It is not really advisable to use any kind of wax or polish on bathroom floors, because they are not water resistant, and will water-mark very quickly.

Gilding

Gilding can be used in a limited way in the bathroom to add a stylish finishing touch, but should be protected carefully. In the case of any decorative gilding on panels (see Koi carp in silver aluminium leaf, page 32), protect this from water with a sheet of glass or perspex. It is inadvisable to have large, exposed areas of gilding (e.g. covering walls), because the metal will react to the damp conditions, and will discolour. Decorative gilding work on small objects, such as picture or mirror frames, should be sealed with white polish shellac and then varnished with acrylic or oil-based varnish in eggshell or gloss sheen. When embellishing small items with gilding wax, apply over a surface previously sealed with acrylic varnish, and keep away from water.

◀ To protect decorated surfaces from moisture, use a sheet of shatterproof, pre-toughened glass (at least 6mm [¼"] thick) or perspex to cover the decorated area. Have the glass or perspex professionally cut to size with holes drilled for dome-headed, plastic-protected mirror screws. Use a waterproof sealant around all edges of the glass. See pages 56–59.

▲ Delicate finishes such as gilding should always be protected by the method described above. See pages 32–35.

Styling and bathroom accessories

When planning your scheme it is wise to have an idea of the finishing touches you are going to use: will the scheme be best complemented with sleek chrome or will glass add extra definition and style to the look? Or would you like a more rustic or simple feel with wood or bamboo? Most decorating styles will be enhanced if you choose the right accessory to go with them.

The focus on bathroom design in recent years has meant that the choices for bath and utility ware, basins, sinks, taps and accessories are virtually limitless. Traditional styles have been given a high quality lease on life, and innovative, sleek new designs have been introduced, accompanied by a vastly improved range of quality materials. To complement this, every imaginable accessory is available in a variety of materials. If you are planning to install a new bath, sink and toilet, choose the style at the same time as you plan your decoration, so that the whole scheme works together. Similarly, if you are fitting new taps or other fixtures, decide on their style before you start, to achieve an integrated final look.

Sinks

As well as white ceramic sinks available in every imaginable style, including the elegant clean lines of simple square sinks, simple, neat bowls and basins are also popular. These attractive alternatives to the somewhat tired and cumbersome pedestal basin are available in a variety of finishes, including glass, frosted resin, stainless steel, ceramic, stoneware and marble. There is a comprehensive range of shelves, countertops and stands to complement them.

▲ Ceramic bowl on reproduction washstand (top), wide square modern ceramic sink (right), glass bowl sink (bottom).

Bathware

Choose a bath from streamlined up-to-the-minute wall-fitted styles, or fashionable, modern, freestanding baths. There are roll-tops for the 21st century or traditional, old-fashioned styles; there are also designer baths in marble, glass and wood, hi-tech Jacuzzis, and spa baths. Good-quality baths are available to suit all budgets, so you can choose either a style that will blend in with your overall scheme or else one that makes a strong statement in itself.

Most baths are made from cast iron, steel, acrylic or more modern stone-cast resin and are available in a variety of shapes, including rectangular, oval, corner and hexagonal. Happily the fashion for strangely coloured bathroom suites seems to have faded into the past, and baths are now usually a clean, simple white, suitable for most decorating schemes. Roll-tops have ready-to-paint exteriors, so that they can be tailored to decorating schemes, and an extensive choice of bath panels is also available.

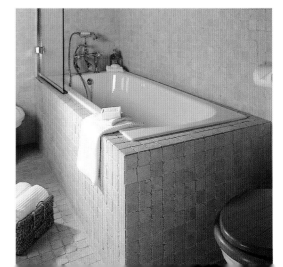

▶ Reproduction cast iron roll-top bath with claw feet (above) and modern steel bath in mosaic surround (below).

◀ Single
monoblock lever

◀ ▲ Traditional tap and
shower mixer (left) and
modern, simple style taps
(above).

Toilets and bidets

An assortment of toilets and bidets are available in
styles that mix and match with all new styles and
innovations for baths and sinks, including modern,
understated styles, and attractive reproductions.

Taps

You can find bathroom taps and mixers in types to
suit all modern and traditional bath and sink styles.
There are ranges of sleek, chrome taps in clean,
simple styles available as basin, bath, wall, and
pillar-mounted single-hole and three-hole sets.
Colour can be introduced by using attractive tap
heads in frosted resin. Comprehensive ranges of
high-quality, traditional designs are also available,
as are showerheads and attachments.

Accessories and bathroom furniture

Mirrors, shelves, bath and shower racks, towel
rails, towel rings and toothbrush and toilet-roll
holders are available in shiny and brushed chrome,
brass, glass, frosted resin, porcelain, stoneware,
and wood. They are designed to blend and
harmonize with bathroom schemes or to stand out
as design features in their own right.

Options for bathroom furniture are equally
diverse. Choose from modern fitted cabinets and
units in many styles and materials, or bathroom
chairs, wash baskets, shelves, and storage units in
rattan or wicker. Cabinets, freestanding units, linen
presses, and armoires in painted or bare wood can
also be considered. The range of options is endless
– mix old with new, ornate with plain, or textured
with smooth.

Add that finishing touch with soft neutral or
coloured towels, toiletries and sundries that
complement your scheme.

Painted bathroom projects

To accentuate the beauty or style
of each scheme, the projects have
been styled and accessorized with
baths, sinks, basins, taps, mirrors
and towel rails in materials that
suit the style of the design.

◀ ▶ A deep freestanding
roll-top bath has been
painted to blend in with the
soft greens of this project
(left – see pages 60–63),
while a beautiful travertine
limestone basin brings out
the beauty of the marble
Trompe L'Oeil bathroom
(right – see pages 76–79).

Blues and Lilacs

At the cool end of the colour spectrum, blue and lilac create a palette that echoes nature's own diversity – the lilac-blushed dawn, watery grey-blue horizons, rich, clear skies, stormy blues, and deepest night-time indigo, reflected in azure and ultramarine seas.

This multi-faceted range is a natural source of inspiration for decorative bathroom schemes. Blue gives a sense of balance and peace – a great colour for rooms where you want to create a feeling of restfulness and relaxation.

Lilac is immediately calming and is said to promote tranquillity and spirituality. Both colours are ideal for creating a place of retreat and contemplation.

From pale tints to strong shades, both blue and lilac work well with white, off-white and silver. Use paler tones for a sense of spaciousness, and darker tones for a more contained atmosphere. As well as being individually versatile, blue and lilac work well together and can produce stunning results when combined with greens and greys, or enhanced with yellows, oranges and pinks.

This beautiful and striking oriental style koi carp design has been applied in silver aluminium leaf giving a really special, highly reflective finish. Excellent for rooms where you want a distinctive, high quality feel.

Koi carp in silver aluminium leaf

Aluminium leaf gives an extremely opulent look here. As an alternative, the mural could be stencilled with brilliant silver spray paint onto a previously varnished base, or another colour combination, such as blue on white.

Where to apply

This large, single-motif koi carp stencil is being used here above a sink most suited to a cloakroom or guest bathroom. For areas subject to more moisture it is advisable to cover the mural with perspex (or thick, safe, shatterproof glass) to give further protection. The koi carp mural will also make a stunning feature wall elsewhere in the room.

Difficulty level: moderate, although the gilding process can take a little time.

YOU WILL NEED:

Koi carp stencil (pages 115 or 124) • white acrylic primer • pale blue matt emulsion paint • acrylic matt varnish • acrylic gloss varnish • gilding size • white polish shellac • aluminium leaf – either loose or transfer leaf • decorator's brushes • varnish brush • gilding mop or soft brush • fitch brush • repositionable spray adhesive • palette or paper plate • high-density foam in 4 cm (1½") squares • kitchen towel • plastic rubber • medium grade sandpaper • spirit level • perspex, or safe, shatterproof glass (if necessary)

PREPARATION

The success of this project will largely depend on the care taken in your preparation, particularly in thoroughly sanding between coats, as the gilded effect works best on a smooth, flat surface. To achieve this, prime the wall with acrylic primer, sand until smooth and wipe off excess dust with a tack cloth. Then paint with two coats of pale blue matt emulsion, sanding and wiping off the dust between coats. Varnish with one coat of acrylic matt varnish.

1 MARKING UP AND STICKING STENCIL IN PLACE

Refer to Stencil Techniques (page 22). Use a spirit level, ruler and pencil to mark several points vertically down the central line of the area to be stencilled.

Use a permanent marker to make some small marks vertically down the centre of the stencil. Apply repositionable spray adhesive to the bottom half of the reverse of the stencil and line up the central point of the fish with the central point of the wall according to the marks you have made. Stick the stencil to the wall. Firmly press all edges of the cut-out areas of the stencil to ensure they are properly stuck down. This will minimize any bleeding.

2 STENCILLING FIRST SECTION

Dip a piece of high-density foam into the gilding size and thoroughly dab off the excess onto a piece of kitchen towel. If there is too much gilding size on the sponge, it will bleed under the edges of the stencil, and the aluminium leaf will stick to this, causing the image to have blurred edges. Lightly stencil the gilding size onto the lower half of the stencil and then carefully peel off the stencil.

The gilding size has a sticking time of about 20–30 minutes, depending on room temperature. If you do not think you can gild half the stencil in that time, work in smaller sections at a time.

3 APPLYING ALUMINIUM LEAF

You can use either loose leaf or transfer leaf. The transfer leaf is easier to handle, but can be more difficult to remove, while the loose leaf tends to be a little more difficult to handle, but is easier to brush away. The overall finish is the same, however.

To prepare the aluminium leaf, first wash your hands to remove any traces of gilding size and then lay out several complete sheets of leaf. Carefully cut some of the sheets in half using clean, sharp scissors.

Lift the leaf onto the sized area and carefully press down, smoothing out with a clean, dry finger to remove wrinkles.

Repeat this process until all of the gilding size has been covered, using the whole sheets for the head, main body section and fish fins and the half pieces for the waves.

4 REMOVING EXCESS LEAF

Once all of the sized area has been covered, smooth your finger over it again to ensure the leaf is completely stuck down, and also to check that no bits of size have been missed.

Use the gilding mop or soft brush to brush over the gilded areas lightly, until the leaf that has not been stuck down starts to dislodge and the clean edges of the image appear. Keep brushing until all of the excess leaf has been removed. Carefully wipe away the excess. It is useful to have a vacuum cleaner on hand to clean up the metallic castings and dust.

5 STENCILLING SECOND SECTION

Apply repositionable spray adhesive to the top half of the reverse of the stencil. Use the original registration guides to line up the stencil carefully. Restick the stencil to the wall, pressing firmly into place, as before. Lightly stencil the gilding size onto the upper half of the stencil and then carefully peel off the stencil.

6 APPLYING ALUMINIUM LEAF

Apply the alminium leaf as before to the sized areas, carefully smoothing out each gilded section with your fingers to ensure it is fully stuck down. Repeat the process until the whole stencil is covered. When the gilding is complete, use the gilding mop or soft brush to brush off the excess alminium leaf gently, as before.

Use a small dry fitch brush to loosen any stubborn pieces of leaf and to neaten up the gilded edges. Use some of the original pale blue matt emulsion to cover any mistakes.

7 FINISHING

Use an rubber to rub off any pencil marks that are still showing. Brush off any loose pieces of rubber and then wipe over the whole surface using a tack cloth to ensure the surface is dust free.

Use a varnish brush to carefully apply a coat of white polish shellac, taking care not to over-brush the shellac, as this will cause a streaky finish. Leave to dry overnight.

Finally, varnish with two coats of acrylic gloss varnish. For areas subject to a lot of splashing, cover the area with a sheet of perspex or safe, shatterproof glass.

This seascape mural will give your creative and imaginative spirit the chance to come to the fore, and an opportunity to bring crystalline, aquamarine, azure seas and white sandy beaches right into your bathroom.

Seascape mural

More of an abstract painting than a beautifully drawn landscape, you do not need to be a fully-fledged artist to get good results here. It's more a chance for you to create a space where you can relax and dream of far-off places.

Where to apply

This mural has been designed to run along the wall behind a bath, but it could equally be adapted as a stunning feature wall or panel. The mural is not suitable for shower areas (see Finishing, step 10).

Difficulty level: moderate, just needs confidence to have a go.

YOU WILL NEED:

Seaside holiday photos • white acrylic paper • mid-blue matt emulsion • ultramarine matt emulsion • bright turquoise matt emulsion • acrylic matt varnish • acrylic eggshell varnish • acrylic scumble glaze • 2 × 60 ml acrylic paints in corresponding colours: ultramarine, bright turquoise, Prussian blue, light turquoise, 1 × 60 ml in ivory, green, sandy cream • artist's gouache or water-colours in primary blue, process cyan, cobalt, ultramarine, Prussian blue, cerulean, white, yellow ochre, viridian • 2½ cm (1"), 5 cm (2") and 10 cm (4") decorator's brushes • fitch brushes in various sizes • artist's sable brushes • hog-hair softener • 7 mm (¼") lining tape • white chalk • A3 (30 × 42 cm/12" × 16½") white watercolour paper • A3 (30 × 42 cm/12" × 16½") tracing paper • spirit level • ruler • set square • pencil • pot for brushes • pot for water • perspex or safe, shatterproof glass (if necessary)

PREPARATION
Prime and then paint the walls in mid-blue matt emulsion, taking care to create as smooth a surface as possible. Varnish the walls with one coat of acrylic matt varnish.

1 SOURCE MATERIAL
You will need photos that have the stunning turquoise and blue colours so prevalent in the seas of the Mediterranean, Caribbean and the Far East. You may want to paint a specific beach that you fell in love with on a particular holiday, or a more general inspiring beach scene – either way, collect together your seascape holiday photos. Additional sources could be postcards and pictures from travel brochures or magazines. Gather all of these into an inspiring montage.

2 WATERCOLOUR SKETCH
Start the artistic flow by painting a watercolour sketch. Use the colours listed above in gouache or watercolour and paint a loose scene on watercolour paper, based on the scenes in your photos. Otherwise you could use my watercolour sketch as a starting inspiration.

MAKING UP THE GRIDS

To enlarge your design you will need to create a grid both on your sketch and on the wall. The area of wall to be painted here is 120 × 90 cm (4' × 3').

Trim your watercolour sketch so that it has the same proportional dimensions as the wall area. Then attach a piece of tracing paper to fit the watercolour and draw a 120 × 90 cm (4' × 3') grid onto it. Divide the wall area into a 120 × 90 cm (4' × 3') grid. Stick 7 mm (⅛") lining tape on the vertical and horizontal lines to make up the grid.

TRANSFERRING THE DESIGN

Use a piece of white chalk to transfer the design onto the wall. Look at the horizon line and sketch in where it is in relation to the upper horizontal line (upper third), the sandbank (middle third) and the shoreline in the foreground (lower third).

Once the chalk sketch is in place, remove the lining tapes. You are now ready to paint.

BLOCKING IN MAIN COLOURS

A blank space can appear a little daunting, so the first stage is to block in all of the main colours. Use large fitch brushes and 5 cm (2") decorator's brushes for larger areas. Start by painting in the main colours for the sea – ultramarine from the sandbank to the horizon, with a streak of turquoise above the sandbank. Then add Prussian blue to the right of the sandbank.

Now add a further line of ultramarine from the shoreline to the right edge of the mural. Paint in the remaining sea area with bright turquoise, and blend the wet edge of the ultramarine with the bright turquoise. Paint the sky in the same turquoise. Then paint in the sandbank and the beach area with the ivory acrylic paint, adding a splash of green to the sand dune on the left. You will have now blocked in all of the main colours and made a very good beginning to the mural painting.

Tip

To create a crisp line for edges on borders: stick painting tape or masking tape along the length of the edge; brush a thin coat of acrylic matt varnish over the edge of the tape, and allow to dry before painting. This will prevent any paint bleeding under the tape, and will give a clean, finished edge.

ADDING DETAIL

Add some more of the light turquoise onto the bright turquoise in the sea at the front just below the ultramarine band, blending the edges as much as possible. Add the same colour to the skyline above the sea horizon line.

7 CREATING THE SHORELINE

Add more of the sandy cream acrylic paint to the sand dune and shoreline to create more textural qualities on the beach, and then add some green to the sand dunes.

8 APPLYING GLAZES

Follow the chart below to make up the two glazes for the next stage. These glazes will be semi-transparent and will have a longer open time than the emulsion base coats, which will allow you to blend the colours together.

Use a 2½ cm (1") decorator's brush or fitch brush to apply layers of the bright turquoise and sea-blue glazes to the sea, using the glazes to blend the light and darker blues. Use a hog-hair softener to feather the two glazes together and remove any streaky paint lines.

Use a 5 cm (2") decorator's brush to apply two layers of the bright turquoise glaze to the sky. Use a hog-hair softener to remove streaky paint lines. On the final glaze brush over the horizon line, blending the sea and sky.

	Glaze 1: Bright turquoise	Glaze 2: Sea blue
1	12½ ml (2½ tbsp) acrylic scumble glaze	12½ ml (2½ tbsp) acrylic scumble glaze
2	4 cm (1½") process cyan gouache, squeezed from the tube	2 cm (¾") Prussian blue gouache, squeezed from the tube
3	Mix thoroughly to disperse paint and remove lumps	Mix thoroughly to disperse paint and remove lumps
4	12½ ml (2½ tbsp) bright turquoise flat latex paint	12½ ml (2½ tbsp) ultramarine flat latex paint
5	15 ml (1 tbsp) acrylic matt varnish	15 ml (1 tbsp) acrylic matt varnish
6	75 ml (5 tsp) water	75 ml (5 tsp) water
7	Mix and cover until ready to use	Mix and cover until ready to use

9 FINAL DETAILS

Once the painting of the sea is complete use a fitch brush to apply a little ivory acrylic paint to add definition to the top of the sandbank and sand dune.

Then use a little of the turquoise glaze, with some water added on a sable or one-stroke brush to run the colour along the shoreline – this will soften the point where the water meets the shore.

10 FINISHING

If the mural is going behind a bath with minimum usage and will not be subject to a great deal of splashing (i.e. occasional baths only), varnish with two coats of acrylic eggshell varnish. For areas subject to more splashing, cover the area with perspex (or thick, safe, shatterproof glass) to protect the mural. This finish is not suitable for shower areas, as water will get behind the perspex covering and will mark the painted surface.

Give your bathroom a touch of style with this elegant damask-effect stencil and classic wood panelling in a modern lavender and metallic colour scheme.

Damask walls

Subtle textural contrasts are achieved by using a highly reflective violet interference paint, which gives glimmering tones of silver and metallic violet – a damask shimmer on soft matt lavender walls. Interference paint makes the lustrous damask effect more obvious and once stencilled, it will appear silver at one angle and a vibrant metallic purple at another.

Where to apply

The two-layer damask stencil used in this project is designed as an all-over wallpaper repeat, which can either be applied throughout or on selected walls above the panelling. The stencil can also be used for a full drop on one or more walls, but allow plenty of time for this. The panelling is perfect for lower walls, at sink height, or under sink units, as well as for bath panels.

Difficulty level: moderate, the repeat stencilling is quite a lengthy process.

Note

Tongue-and-groove panelling is not difficult in itself to fit, but creating a secure backing baton system to attach the wood to and cutting wood to fit around doors, windows and recesses can be difficult, and does require reasonable carpentry skills. I suggest you seek professional help in panelling the room, or if you are keen on DIY use a comprehensive DIY manual to guide you through the important stages. The face-nailing technique is explained in this project for enthusiasts.

Painted tongue-and-groove

YOU WILL NEED:

10 cm (4") beaded tongue-and-groove timber to cover the area to be panelled • 4 cm (1½") OG moulding or dado to run across top of panelling • 15 cm (6") board moulding for room or panelled areas only • wood filler • knotting solution • methylated spirits • white acrylic primer • lavender matt emulsion • acrylic eggshell varnish • acrylic matt varnish • decorator's brushes • fitch brush • 2½ cm (1") nails • nail punch • hammer • palette knife • sanding block • dusting brush

1 FACE-NAILING TECHNIQUE

This project uses 10 cm (4") beaded tongue-and-groove panelling. As the panelling is to be painted, the tongue-and-groove boards can be attached to the backing batons using the face-nailing technique. For wood that is to be left bare, varnished or stained, the secret-nailing technique should be used – refer to a comprehensive DIY manual for details.

Attach the tongue-and-groove boards to the backing baton using small 2½ cm (1") nails. Sink the nail heads into the wood using a nail punch. Fill these holes with wood filler and sand when dry. Brush off any dust particles.

2 ADDING MOULDING AND SKIRTING

The moulding and skirting board should be joined to the top and bottom of the panelled areas at this stage and prepared and painted in the same way as the panelling (see Finishing Touches).

3 PREPARATION FOR PAINTING

Once the wood panelling has been fitted, use a fitch brush to apply knotting solution to all visible knots to avoid any discolouration from resin. Clean the brush with methylated spirits immediately. Prime the wood with one coat of acrylic primer. Make sure that you push the primer into the beaded joins to achieve full coverage.

4 PAINTING AND VARNISHING BEADED PANELLING

Apply two coats of lavender matt emulsion to the paneled walls allowing plenty of drying time between coats for the paint to dry out in the beaded joins.

Make up a combined varnish mixture using ⅔ acrylic matt varnish and ⅓ acrylic eggshell varnish, and apply two coats to the panelled area. This will dry with a very slight sheen, which will complement the damask stencilled walls, but still have a near matt finish, particularly attractive on wooden panelling.

Damask stencil

YOU WILL NEED:

Two-layer damask repeat stencil (pages 114 or 124) • white acrylic primer • pale lavender matt emulsion • acrylic matt varnish • acrylic eggshell varnish (if necessary) • violet interference paint for stencilling • violet metallic stencil paint • repositionable spray adhesive • masking tape • divided palette or paper plate • high-density foam in 4 cm (1½") squares • kitchen towel • spirit level • ruler • pencil • plastic rubber • set square • permanent marker • scalpel or craft knife • hairdryer (if necessary) • tack cloth

PREPARATION

Apply one coat of white acrylic primer to the walls to be stencilled. Sand, and then paint with two coats of pale lavender matt emulsion. Varnish with two coats of acrylic matt varnish.

MARKING UP FOR STENCILLING

Refer to Stencil Techniques (page 22). Use the ruler, pencil and spirit level to make guide marks horizontally along the top of the wall and vertically down the left-hand side of the wall. Use the permanent marker, set square and ruler to draw a horizontal and vertical line onto the stencil. If the stencil does not have registration dots in the corners, place the second-layer stencil on the first-layer stencil, so that all motifs line up, and cut registration dots in the corners.

1 POSITIONING STENCIL AND STENCILLING FIRST REPEAT

Spray repositionable adhesive on the reverse of the first-layer stencil and position the stencil in the top left-hand corner of the wall.

Spoon a good amount of the violet interference paint into a divided palette or onto a paper plate and apply using the high-density foam. You will need to apply three layers of the paint to achieve its full effect.

Apply a thin first coat of paint in light, sweeping motions over the stencil. Leave to dry. Apply the second layer using a little more paint, but wiping over the stencil in the same way. For the third coat, stipple the sponge onto the wall to create a slightly textured effect. Use a pencil to make a light mark on the wall through the registration dots.

To create a more obvious effect, stencil the first coat with the lavender matt emulsion used for the panelling. Then apply two layers of violet interference paint.

2 STENCILLING REMAINING DROP

Remove the stencil and line up below the first repeat using the vertical marks on the wall and the line on your stencil. Place the stencil underneath the first motif so that the pattern motifs have the same amount of distance on the horizontal join as within the pattern itself. Use the permanent marker to draw around some of the flower petals from the first repeat that you can see through the Mylar. These will act as your registration guides. Press the stencil firmly to the wall.

Repeat the stencilling process as for the first repeat. Continue working down the wall until you have completed the drop, bending the Mylar up on the last repeat if necessary.

3 STENCILLING SECOND AND REMAINING DROPS

Line the stencil up to the right of the first repeat so that the horizontal marks on the wall correspond with the horizontal line on the stencil. Position the stencil so that the pattern motifs have the same amount of distance on the vertical join as they do within the pattern itself. As before, draw some of the flower petals from the first repeat onto the Mylar, this time on the left-hand side, to act as registration guides for further repeats. You will now have drawn registration guides on both the left-hand side and top of the stencil. Repeat the stencilling process as before; remove the stencil, place directly beneath this repeat, and continue stencilling.

4 POSITIONING AND STENCILLING SECOND LAYER

Apply repositionable spray to the reverse of the second-layer stencil and use the registration dots cut in the Mylar to position the stencil correctly. Press the stencil down firmly. Pour some of the violet metallic stencil paint into the palette and stencil using the high-density foam. The details on this layer should be subtle and not overstated.

Repeat this process until layer two has been applied to all the stencilled areas.

5 FINISHING TOUCHES

Rub off all pencil marks. The upper wall should not need varnishing again, as the metallic paint has a highly non-absorbent protective surface. However, for bathrooms with extremely high moisture levels, apply a coat of acrylic eggshell varnish, although this will reduce the contrast between the paints, reducing the damask effect.

Finally, use some of the violet metallic stencil paint to paint lightly over the moulding and skirting board at the top and bottom of the panelling. This attractive finishing touch will bring the whole scheme together.

Create this simple, yet undeniably bold, striking and modern look in several easy steps.

Soft vertical stripes

This project has the bonus of giving that feeling of extra height to rooms with low ceilings. It's great for a room where you want to create real impact.

Where to apply

Use as a striking feature wall or throughout a room.

Difficulty level: **easy, but tearing the tapes is time-consuming so allow plenty of preparation time.**

YOU WILL NEED:

White acrylic primer • mid-tone lilac matt emulsion • acrylic matt varnish • brilliant silver spray paint or silver metallic emulsion • painting tape or self-adhesive brown paper tape • wide low-tack masking tape • decorator's brushes • fitch brush • spirit level • ruler • pencil • plastic rubber • protective mask and goggles

PREPARATION

Prime and then paint walls with two coats of mid-tone lilac matt emulsion, taking care to create as smooth a surface as possible. Varnish the walls with two coats of acrylic matt varnish. The two coats of varnish used here will also act as the final coat.

1 MARKING UP THE WALL

Use a ruler and pencil to mark up distances of 5 cm (2") and 15 cm (6") horizontally across the wall to create the spacing for the vertical stripes. Use the spirit level to ensure the marks make up vertical lines.

2 TEARING TAPE

Count the number of lengths of painting tape you will need to cover the wall, based on two per silver stripe. Cut the appropriate number of lengths of tape adding on approximately 5 cm (2") to each length.

To tear the tape for creating the soft edge for the stripes, take the tape between the thumbs of each hand and tear a 1 cm (½") wide strip off the sticky edge. Try to keep the torn line roughly straight, but do not worry if it is slightly wobbly or if you have to start the line again, the overall impression will be of a soft edge. You might want to practise on a shorter length of tape first to master tearing it.

3 ATTACHING THE TAPE

To stick the torn tape into place to create the outlines for the soft stripes, stick the tape to the wall so that the torn edges are to the left and right of each 5 cm (2") stripe. You will find that as the tape has a torn irregular edge you cannot stick it directly onto the pencil marks – use them as a guide to keep the tape running straight. To ensure the lines are truly vertical, regularly place the spirit level on the outer straight edge of the tape to check it is running straight and alter as necessary.

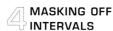

4 MASKING OFF INTERVALS

Use the wide low-tack masking tape (or more painting tape) to mask off the intervals between the torn-edge stripes. Ensure the lilac paintwork is covered to prevent any silver getting onto these areas.

5 ANTI-BLEED TECHNIQUE

Press the edges of the torn tape firmly onto the wall. Use a fitch brush to brush some acrylic matt varnish over the edge of the tape onto the lilac beneath and allow to dry.

Safety note

Always allow good ventilation while working.

6 SPRAYING FIRST COAT OF SILVER

Wearing the protective mask and goggles and ensuring there is as much ventilation in the room as possible, spray the silver paint between the torn strips. Hold the can about 20–30 cm (8"–12") away from the wall and spray a light film onto the wall. Shake the spray can vigorously at regular intervals to relieve any clogging of the nozzle. It is better to spray lightly over the same area repeatedly rather than attempting to spray a thick coat onto the wall, as that would cause the paint to run. As soon as you have finished spraying, leave the room, shutting the door behind you so that the fumes will escape through the window.

If you prefer not to use spray paint, a similar effect can be achieved using silver metallic emulsion. Although this will not have the odour problems, it will not create the same degree of brilliance. Silver emulsion will have a silver lustre, which at many angles of the light will appear grey. The brilliant silver spray paint has a higher lustre and does not appear dark from many angles.

7 SPRAYING A SECOND COAT

Allow the wall to dry for 30 minutes and apply a second coat of silver. Again spray an even, thin coat and build this up until a brilliant silver effect has been achieved. Leave the room again for 30 minutes.

8 REMOVING TAPES

Carefully peel away all of the tape on the wall to reveal the stripes. They will be brilliant silver, but with a pleasing soft edge.

9 FINISHING & STYLING

Allow the spray paint to dry for two hours, then use a plastic rubber to rub off any visible pencil marks and use a brush to remove any pieces of rubber. It is not necessary to apply a further coat of varnish as the lilac areas have already been varnished and the silver spray does not need varnishing. However, leave the paint on the wall to harden fully for 24 hours before using the room.

Further accentuate the textural contrast between the smooth, shiny silver paint and the soft matt lilac emulsion by using accessories that also have this implicit textural contrast – such as chrome and silver fixtures and fittings, metallic fabrics and softer items such as towels.

Blues & lilacs variations

Sea-theme paper collage

These collages are effective hung in groups on bright blue- or turquoise-painted walls. Tear strips of coloured sugar paper, wrapping paper or paper from magazines. Use PVA to stick onto firm backing cardboard. Use blue for the sky, turquoise for the sea and beige for the beach. Add cut-out details of boats or seagulls. Dry, and then trim the edges. Flatten under a weight for 24 hours. Stick onto MDF blocks or inside clip frames.

Dragonfly motif

Delicate motifs such as birds and insects are ideal on white cotton voile or painted walls. Make up a curtain (refer to Striped shower curtain, page 100, and to Modern Swedish style, page 60, for making up table and printing on fabric). Prime, paint and varnish walls. Use pale blue stencil paint for the first layer, overprinting the wing tips with mid-blue. Stencil at 23 cm (9") intervals to form a diamond pattern. Add a small leaf motif between the dragonflies. Stencil the second layer using cobalt blue.

Rope spirals

Textured silver spirals on pale blue walls are effective. Cut 25 cm (10") and 30 cm (12") lengths of 7 mm (¼") rope/cord. Prime two pieces of 13 cm (5") square cardboard. Apply a circle of adhesive to each. Wind the rope around itself and press into the glue. Seal the edge and centre with PVA. Make registration marks in a diamond pattern onto primed, painted and varnished walls. Use silver stamp or stencil paint to print the stamps over the marks.

Koi carp and water lily mural

This is an example of how reflective metallic colours can create a stunning feature wall. Prime and paint the walls with pale lilac flat matt emulsion and seal with two coats of acrylic matt varnish. Position and stick your stencil onto the wall. Stencil your design using lilac and mid-green stencil paint; overprint with copper, purple and jade metallic stencil paints (refer to Dolphin mosaic splashback, page 56).

Contemporary squares

Harmonizing tones of purple create this striking design. Cut three sets of three wavy-edged Mylar squares in diminishing sizes. Paint the wall with rich purple matt emulsion. Stick the three largest squares in a vertical column on the wall. Seal edges with varnish. Paint inside the squares with lilac matt emulsion. When dry, stick three middle-sized squares inside the first, seal the edges, and paint with mid-tone purple. Repeat for the smallest squares using rich purple. Apply two coats of varnish to the wall.

Toile du Jouy

This high quality traditional scheme looks stunning both on walls and on fabric for shower curtains and blinds. The design is complex, but demonstrates the level of quality that can be achieved with stencilling techniques. Prime and paint the walls with ivory matt emulsion, and varnish with one coat of acrylic matt varnish. Stencil the whole design with denim blue stencil paint, overprinting the edges of the motifs to give depth. Follow guidelines for wallpaper effect repeat stencilling in Damask walls (page 40). Finally seal with one coat of acrylic matt varnish.

Aquas and Greens

The natural world provides a wealth of possibilities for bathroom colour schemes. The first glimpses of spring, leafy glades, mountain streams, waterfalls and ocean spray produce a refreshing sense of well-being and invigoration. The aquas and greens palette is both refreshing and invigorating, as well as healing and restful.

Aqua and turquoise evoke the feeling of water and its reviving properties. Pale shades create an atmosphere of spaciousness, and will be further enhanced by incorporating reflective glass and metallic finishes. Brighter tones will give a sense of richness and invigoration.

The green palette is naturally harmonious and restful. Use a cool, muted tone-on-tone scheme to create an atmosphere that will soothe and repair, or use zesty accents of lime to rejuvenate and restore the senses. Aqua and green have a timelessness and freshness that means they work well in both modern and classic decorative schemes.

This simple and effective use of glass, faux etching and a metallic finish gives a contemporary feel that is both delicate and stylish. The reflective metallic and glass surfaces create a real sense of spaciousness in the room.

Etched glass squares

Three graceful etched feather motifs are repeated onto 12 glass squares and mounted as an elegant block.

Where to apply
This effect works best as a decorative panel or feature wall in the bathroom.

Difficulty level: moderate.

PREPARATION
Prepare the walls to be painted with metallic emulsion as thoroughly as possible to create a really smooth surface, as reflective metallic finishes show up any lumps and bumps. Prime the walls with white acrylic primer, then paint with two coats of pale aqua matt emulsion, sanding lightly between coats. Allow to dry thoroughly, and then sand again lightly.

> ## YOU WILL NEED:
>
> Feather stencils (pages 119 or 124) • twelve 4 mm (³⁄₁₆") thick polished glass squares each measuring 30 × 30 cm (12" × 12") • twelve 2 mm (¹⁄₁₆") thick MDF squares each measuring 30 × 30 cm (12" × 12") pre-cut at wood yard • white acrylic primer • pale aqua matt emulsion • pale aqua metallic latex paint or acrylic metallic varnish • pale turquoise matt emulsion • three cans glass etching or glass frosting spray • one can white matte spray paint • decorator's brushes • 10 cm (4") synthetic paintbrush • 14 mm (½") lining or edging tape • repositionable spray adhesive • methylated spirits or glass cleaner • tube of extra-strong clear adhesive • strong bonding adhesive pads or fixings for 12 squares • sanding block • tack cloth • kitchen towel • newspaper or other protective paper • protective mask and goggles • scalpel or craft knife • piece of high-density foam • spirit level • ruler • book, or other weight

1 APPLYING METALLIC PAINT
Ensure the final surface is clear of all dust particles by wiping with a tack cloth. Use a 10 cm (4") synthetic paintbrush (or as large as you can manage) to apply the pale aqua metallic emulsion. Metallic varnish can be used if metallic paint is not obtainable. Simply brush over the pale aqua paint base. Paint the wall in sections. Apply a generous amount of paint to each section.

Finish each section by laying off the paint in long, smooth, vertical strokes, working in one direction. All brushstrokes will show up on the reflective finish when it is dry, so finishing in one direction gives the smoothest finish possible. Allow the paint to cure fully for at least 48 hours before fixing the glass squares to the walls.

2 PREPARING GLASS SQUARES AND APPLYING TAPE BORDER
Clean both sides of each of the 12 glass squares using some kitchen towel and methylated spirits or glass cleaner. Use the 14 mm (½") lining or edging tape to create a border on each square. Stick the tape 7 mm (¼") in from each edge, making sure that all of the corners are neat and that the tape is fully stuck down.

3 POSITIONING REVERSE STENCILS

Refer to Stencil Techniques (page 22). This project uses three different feather stencil motifs. You will need four finished etched squares of each motif. Spray repositionable adhesive onto the reverse of the feather stencils and stick in the centre of each taped-off glass square. Take care to position the motifs the same on each square.

4 APPLYING SPRAY AND BUILDING UP THE ETCHED EFFECT

Work outside or in a well-ventilated room. Lay the prepared glass squares on newspaper or other protective paper. Shake the can of etching or frosting spray vigorously and, holding it about 30 cm (12") above the glass, spray a fine even layer of etching spray over the glass squares.

At five-minute intervals, spray a further two coats of etching spray onto the glass squares, regularly shaking the can to prevent the nozzle clogging. To increase the opacity of the etched effect, spray a very light coat of white matt spray paint over the glass squares.

Repeat this whole process applying three more layers of etching spray and one more layer of white spray paint, leaving five minutes between coats.

Finally spray a further two coats of etching spray onto the glass squares.

5 REMOVING TAPES AND STENCIL MOTIF

Allow the glass squares to dry for a couple of hours and then carefully remove the tape and stencil motif from the glass; use the point of a scalpel or craft knife to lift the tip of the feather and carefully pull the stencil away from the glass. To ensure the tape does not pull any of the etched effect away, carefully peel the tape back on itself, not at an angle.

6 PAINTING BACKING SQUARES

Backing squares are used behind the frosted glass squares to provide an easy surface to attach to the wall and to enable the etched effect to become more pronounced.

Use the sanding block to sand each of the MDF squares. Prime with a coat of white acrylic primer. Sand until smooth, and then paint with two coats of the pale turquoise matt emulsion. These squares need to have a smooth surface. To achieve this, paint the edges of the squares first, then rest the square on a slightly raised surface and brush in all directions until the square is covered. Carefully lay off the paint in even strokes working in one direction.

7 PREPARING FOR STICKING AND APPLYING GLUE

Leave both the etched glass squares and the backing squares to dry fully overnight. Ensure they are both clear of dust and particles. Then, working on four squares at a time, carefully squeeze a thin line of extra-strong clear adhesive around the outer edge of the backing squares. Leave this for 2–3 minutes to form a slight skin.

8 STICKING SQUARES TOGETHER

The glass squares are stuck down so that the smooth glass side is exposed. This will mean that the outer side is moisture resistant and the etched side is protected against the wall.

Carefully place the glass square directly over the backing square. Press down firmly all the way around the glass and remove any excess glue with a piece of cardboard or a knife. Cover each square with a piece of kitchen towel and place a heavy object carefully onto the glass to weight it down while the glue hardens overnight. Repeat the process for all 12 squares.

▼ Layout diagram

9 MOUNTING SQUARES ONTO WALL

Remove any fingerprints or greasy marks with methylated spirits or glass cleaner.

Following the layout plan to the left, attach the glass squares to the wall in a grid of 12, using either strong-bonding sticky pads or other glass fixings. Space the glass squares so that there is a 3–5 cm (1¼"–2") gap between each square. Whichever size gap you choose (this may vary depending on the scale of the wall you are mounting them onto), ensure that each gap is exactly the same size throughout.

This stunning mosaic splashback and tile effect has been created using a beautiful dolphin one-layer stencil and jewel-like, hand-painted tiles that imitate the expensive glass and metallic tiles that are becoming so popular.

Dolphin mosaic splashback and hand-painted tiles

This effect will create a unique personal touch and high-quality finish at a fraction of the cost of real mosaic and shop-bought tiles.

Where to apply

The stencil and tiles in this project have been designed to be used in conjunction with each other as a splashback for a sink, but could equally be used as a mural above tiles on a feature wall, or the tiles could be used as part of a tiled wall in their own right – pick and choose to get the look you want. Speciality tile paints are used in this project, which means the finished baked tiles can be used in wet areas, making them especially suitable for walls and splashback areas (although areas subject to constant wetness, such as showers, are not recommended).

Difficulty level: moderate, although completing the project is quite time-consuming.

YOU WILL NEED:

Dolphin mosaic stencil (pages 116 or 124) • white acrylic primer • turquoise matt emulsion • acrylic matt varnish • acrylic eggshell varnish • stencil paint in white, cobalt, sea green, orange, lilac, mid-blue, pale turquoise, bright turquoise • metallic stencil paint in pale green, emerald green, sea green, blue, turquoise, purple, gold, orange, silver, pearl • glitter stencil paints in gold and sea green • decorator's brushes • repositionable spray adhesive • paper plate or palette • high-density foam in 4 cm (1½") squares • kitchen towel • spirit level • pencil • ruler • permanent marker • plastic rubber • tack cloth • perspex or safe, shatterproof glass

SPLASHBACK

PREPARATION

Prime and then paint the walls with two coats of turquoise matt emulsion, taking care to create as smooth a surface as possible. Varnish the walls with one coat of acrylic matt varnish.

1 MARKING UP AND SECURING STENCIL

Refer to Stencil Techniques (page 22). Use a spirit level, ruler and pencil to mark up several points vertically down the central line of the area to be stencilled. Use a permanent marker to make some small marks on the stencil vertically down the centre. Apply repositionable spray adhesive to the reverse of the stencil and line up the central point of the mosaic design with the central point of the wall according to the marks you have made, and stick to the wall. Use the spirit level to check that the design is horizontal.

Firmly press all edges of the cut-out areas of the stencil to ensure they are properly stuck down. This will minimize any bleeding.

2 STENCILLING FIRST STAGE

The best effect with this design is achieved by building up layers of colour to create the depth and richness of true mosaic.

Pour out a small amount of the stencil colours listed above into a divided palette or onto a paper plate.

Apply stencil paints using the guidelines in Stencil Techniques (page 22). Start with the white for the mosaic bubbles. Use pale turquoise and blue for the top and bottom parts of the dolphins, and pale green and blue for the water.

3 ADDING DEFINITION

Stencil bright turquoise to the tops of the dolphins' backs and more white and blue to the lower parts of their bodies to create light and dark shadows. Add orange to the line of mosaic running along the centre of the bodies.

4 THE WAVES AND BORDER

Fill up the whole mosaic around the dolphins in blues, turquoises, greens and a little lilac creating lighter and darker areas on the waves. Stencil the border using the colours you have used so far.

5 METALLIC COLOURS

Pour out a small amount of the pale green, emerald green, sea green, pale turquoise, mid-blue, purple, gold, orange and silver metallic colours, as well as some pearl stencil paint into a divided palette or onto a paper plate. Metallic stencil paint goes a long way, so you will not need much of each colour. Stencil the corresponding metallic colours over the original colours. Add pale turquoise and mid-blue over the top of the backs, and silver and pearl to the lower bodies. Add metallic orange and gold over the orange stripe running along the bodies.

6 WATER AND WAVES

Add the metallic blues, greens and pearl, and use the purple metallic paint to wash over some of the sea colours.

7 ADDING GLITTER HIGHLIGHTS

To add extra richness to the design, use stencil glitter paints in gold and sea green. To use the glitter paint, use a small brush to paint it onto your sponge and then stencil directly onto the wall. Build layers for a solid metal effect or stencil lightly for a dusting of glitter. Use sea green to highlight the dolphins' eyes and the top of their backs and gold for the line running through their middles and for some of the border.

8 FINISHING

Peel back the stencil to reveal the rich and diverse colours in your mosaic splashback. Use a rubber to rub off any visible pencil marks. Brush off any loose pieces of rubber and then wipe over the whole surface using a tack cloth to ensure the surface is dust-free. Then seal the splashback stencil with two coats of acrylic eggshell varnish. For areas subject to heavy splashing, cover the area with perspex (or thick, safe, shatterproof glass) to protect the splashback.

TILES

YOU WILL NEED:

Twenty 10 × 10 cm (4" × 4") plain white ceramic tiles • porcelain paint in orange, turquoise, blue, green and gold (see Resource Directory) • relief porcelain liner in gold, copper and silver • glass gel paint in bright blue and iridescent blue • high-density foam cut to 4 cm (1½") squares • waterproof adhesive • waterproof grout • palette knife • palette or paper plate • kitchen towel • artist's sable brush • small ruler and pencil • fine felt-tipped pen • 2½ cm (1") low-tack masking tape • methylated spirits • spirit level • scalpel or craft knife

PREPARATION

Clean the tiles with methylated spirits to ensure a grease-free surface.

1 MARKING UP AND MASKING OFF

Use a fine felt-tipped pen and ruler to mark up a 3 cm (1¼") square in the centre of each tile – this will act as a guide at a later stage. Cut two pieces of 2½ cm (1") wide low-tack masking tape to fit exactly inside the marked-up square and stick securely. Mask off each tile in this way.

2 SPONGING FIRST COLOUR

Pour a little bright orange porcelain paint into a palette and dip a piece of high-density foam into the paint. Sponge onto two of the tiles, covering the whole surface. Repeat this process for all 20 tiles using the turquoise, blue and green porcelain paints. Apply the different colours to the tiles in even numbers, so that they can be paired when you come to mount them.

3 SPONGING SECOND COLOUR

Allow the paint to dry for several hours, and then lightly sponge the gold porcelain paint in the same way over the orange. Handle carefully, as the orange paint will only be partially dry. Gold has been applied to soften the orange so that it blends well with the other colours and to give a metallic lustre. Add a second coat of turquoise, blue and green to the remaining tiles if you want to increase the colour depth. Leave to dry for two hours and then carefully remove the masking-tape squares using a scalpel or craft knife. Allow to dry thoroughly overnight.

4 APPLYING PORCELAIN LINER

Gold and copper porcelain liner is used on one tile, and silver and gold on the other. Gently squeeze the paste onto your pre-marked lines. Apply a second square, using copper inside the gold, and gold inside the silver. Allow to dry for 24–48 hours. For the gold and copper tile, apply further squares of gold and copper. When the liner forms a skin, dab a pool of gold porcelain paint into the tile centre using an artist's sable brush. Leave to dry for a further 24–48 hours. Apply the process to all of the tiles, varying the colours used.

5 BAKING THE TILES

Place the tiles onto the oven shelf, and set the temperature to 150°C (300°F). When the oven is hot enough, bake for 35 minutes, then open the oven door and allow to cool. Follow the paint manufacturer's guidelines. You will find that the paste colours have blended and may have formed attractive bubbles on their surfaces.

6 APPLYING GLASS GEL PAINT

For the tiles with blank centres, apply the gel paint. Squeeze a small amount of bright blue gel into the central square and smooth with a palette knife. Remove any gel on the liner with a sable brush.

Leave to dry for a couple of hours and then apply the iridescent blue gel in the same way. Allow to dry overnight. The gel will dry to a hard resin.

7 FINISHING

The finished tiles should be left for a couple of days to harden. They are then ready to mount around the mosaic. Use waterproof adhesive and grout and a spirit level to ensure the tiles are vertical.

Create a calm, restful space with this modern Swedish style bathroom where both traditional elements and simple, modern motifs and colours are combined effectively to create a harmonized and balanced feel.

Modern Swedish style

Note
Refer to page 40 for advice on constructing tongue-and-groove panelling.

Thick flooring tongue-and-groove is used to create a truly Scandinavian look for the walls, and close-toned moss-greens give a sense of restful coordination. The delicate, hand-printed sheer fabric keeps the look light and airy.

Where to apply

This is a theme for the whole room – the wood panelling can be used throughout or on main walls and always looks good for bath panels, especially if you are not using a roll-top bath as here. The printed square pictures and sheer fabric can be used as feature items as appropriate.

Difficulty level: **moderate.**

Painted Tongue-and-Groove

YOU WILL NEED:

15 cm (6") flooring tongue-and-groove timber to cover the area to be panelled • wood filler • knotting solution • methylated spirits • white acrylic primer • pale moss-green matt emulsion • acrylic matt varnish • decorator's brushes • fitch brush • palette knife • sanding block • dusting brush

1 PREPARING PANELLING

This project uses 15 cm (6") flooring tongue-and-groove with joints that fit snugly together. Once the wood panelling has been constructed on your chosen walls, fill and sand any nail holes or cracks in the wood (refer to

Damask Walls, page 40). Remove dust with a dusting brush.

Apply knotting solution using a fitch brush to all visible knots to prevent future discolouration from resin. Clean the brush with methylated spirits immediately after use.

2 APPLYING PRIMER

Prime the wood with one coat of acrylic primer. As the joins on the wood are close-fitting take care not to clog them up with paint, so apply the primer lightly over the wood joins. When the primer has dried, use the sanding block to lightly sand the wood to remove any roughness or small lumps that have come up from painting. Dust off with a dusting brush or dry paintbrush.

3 PAINTING TONGUE-AND-GROOVE

Apply two coats of pale moss-green matt emulsion. Before the paint dries, run a palette knife down the joins of the wood to remove any paint and keep them open. When the paint has fully dried apply two coats of acrylic matt varnish.

Decorative Squares

PREPARATION

Lightly sand each MDF square. Remove dust and prime with one coat of white acrylic primer, then paint with two base coats of pale moss-green matt emulsion. Allow to dry (refer to painting backing squares, step 6, in Etched Glass Squares, page 54). Using a ruler and pencil, mark up a 14 cm (5½") square in the middle of each painted MDF square, and mask off the inner square using low-tack masking tape. Varnish the edge of the tape.

YOU WILL NEED:

Wild parsley stencil (pages 118 or 124) • three 15 mm (⅝") thick MDF squares each measuring 30 × 30 cm (12" × 12") • mid-tone moss-green flat latex paint • pale moss-green matt emulsion • stencil paints in pale green, leaf-green, dark leaf-green and ivory • white acrylic primer • matt acrylic varnish • decorator's brushes • fitch brush • sanding block • low-tack masking tape • painting tape • repositionable spray adhesive • divided palette or paper plate • high-density foam in 4 cm (1½") squares • kitchen towel • ruler • pencil • tack cloth • screw eyes and picture wire

1 ADDING SECOND BASE COLOUR

Once the varnish is dry, paint the outside of the squares, including the outer return, with two coats of the mid-tone moss-green matt emulsion.

Carefully remove the masking tape and varnish the whole of each square.

2 POSITIONING STENCILS

Refer to Stencil Techniques (page 22). This simple wild parsley stencil is designed as a continuous motif that carries on vertically over each of the three squares. To position the stencils, lay out the three painted squares in a vertical column, spray repositionable adhesive onto the reverse of each stencil and position them on each square making sure that the design lines up square to square.

3 STENCILLING WILD PARSLEY MOTIF AND ADDING DETAIL

Pour a little pale green, leaf-green, dark leaf-green and ivory stencil paints into a divided palette or onto a paper plate, and stencil the whole of each motif with the leaf-green. Apply patches of the pale green to the flower heads and some leaves on each square.

Stencil ivory onto the very tips of some of the leaves and around the edges of the flower heads on each square. When this has dried, stencil the dark leaf-green onto the very tips of the flower heads, the stems at the centre of the flower heads, and some of the leaves.

4 VARNISHING STENCILLED SQUARES

Allow each square to dry thoroughly and then varnish with one coat of acrylic matt varnish. Carefully attach two screw eyes to the back of each square and add picture wire for hanging. Otherwise, rout out a hole in the top centre back of each square and hang.

Hand-Printed Curtain

PREPARATION

To make up a simple sheer curtain for printing, first measure the width and drop of your window. The width of the fabric should be 1½ times the width of the window; the length should be that of the finished drop plus another 10 cm (4") for turning up a double hem at each end. When you have cut the fabric to the right size, turn the top, and bottom edges over twice. Pin, machine-sew the hem, and press.

1 STICKING FABRIC TO TABLE

Lay the bubble wrap and lining paper widthwise over a tabletop or counter and secure with masking tape. Use the ruler and pencil to draw a line 1 cm (½") horizontally across the edge of the lining paper. Line up the bottom hem of the curtain with the line you have drawn, and stick the fabric down with masking tape.

2 POSITIONING THE STENCIL AND STENCILLING FIRST REPEAT

Apply repositionable spray adhesive to the reverse of the stencil. Use a permanent marker to draw a line at the bottom of the design, line this up with the top edge of the masking tape, and stick the motif onto the curtain at the left edge. Pour a little pale green, leaf-green and dark leaf-green stencil paint into a divided palette or paper plate and lightly stencil the whole motif with the leaf-green. Then stencil pale green onto the flower heads and leaves. Add the dark leaf-green to the stems and some of the leaves. Hold the fabric firmly and carefully peel back the stencil. Smooth out the fabric before positioning the next repeat.

3 STENCILLING REMAINING REPEATS

Position the next repeat to the right of the first printed motif leaving approximately the same gap between the flower stems as in the design itself – this will give a feeling of continuity.

Continue the stencilling process, repeating the same colours on each motif until you have covered the width of the fabric.

4 FINISHING

To bring out the beauty of your hand-printed curtain sew a green trim to the bottom edge. Select a heading to hang the curtain, such as Velcro, tab tops or no-sew curtain clips.

Roll-Top Bath

If you are using a roll-top bath, paint the sides in a toning green to fit the overall scheme or a contrasting colour, such as black.

The combination of this beautiful, subtly toned tiled splashback and decorative wide-framed mirror creates an atmosphere of simple cleanliness.

Leaf spatter

Soft greens and ivory are used here in a fine veil of spattered colour and a simple leaf motif, which uses both positive and negative images. The result is pleasingly uncluttered and modern in its simplicity.

Where to apply

The tiles are ideal as a splashback for a sink or would work equally well as a tile border or decorative tile panel. The mirror frame would lend itself to any appropriate placing within the overall context of this room theme.

Difficulty level: moderate.

PREPARATION

Prepare the wall to be used by first priming with white acrylic primer and then painting with two coats of pale green matt emulsion. When the paint has dried, paint a band of ivory matt emulsion around the wall. Use a spirit level, ruler and pencil to make guide marks for two horizontal lines, one at the top of where the tiles are to be mounted, and the other 8 cm (3⅛") above the first. Mask off the rest of the wall with low-tack masking tape, and varnish to prevent bleeding. Paint the band between the tapes with two to three coats of ivory matt emulsion. Remove the tapes and varnish the whole wall with two coats of acrylic eggshell varnish.

Sand the mirror or picture frame. Use white acrylic primer to prime the frame and then paint the whole frame with the ivory matt emulsion, including the recesses and sides. Allow this to dry and then paint a pale green band at the top and bottom of the frame by sticking low-tack masking tape horizontally under the line created by the inner recesses of the mirror. Seal with acrylic matt varnish and then paint the upper and lower bands with two coats of pale green matt emulsion. Varnish the whole frame with acrylic eggshell varnish.

YOU WILL NEED:

Leaf stencils and leaf border stencils (pages 119 or 124) • six 15 × 20 cm (6" × 8") plain ivory tiles • a wide-framed wooden mirror or picture frame • mirror glass to fit frame • porcelain paints in white, mid-green, olive green, dark green and gold • stencil paints in white, mid-green, olive-green, pale green, dark green and gold • porcelain paint thinner • ivory matt emulsion • white acrylic primer • acrylic matt varnish • acrylic eggshell varnish • methylated spirits • waterproof tiling adhesive and waterproof grout • decorator's brushes • fitch brush • stencil brushes • repositionable spray adhesive • painting tape • sanding block • divided palette or paper plate • high-density foam in 4 cm (1½") squares • kitchen towel • disposable surgical or rubber gloves (optional) • clingfilm • low-tack masking tape • spirit level • ruler • pencil • newspaper or other protective paper • hairdryer (if necessary)

1 CLEANING TILES AND PREPARING PORCELAIN PAINTS

Use kitchen paper and methylated spirits to remove any grease or dust from the tiles.

Pour a little of the white, mid-green and olive green porcelain paints into a divided palette or onto a paper plate. Add the porcelain paint thinner until the paint has the consistency of single cream. Mix the paint and thinner using a small fitch brush. The paints are now ready for spattering.

2 ALL-OVER SPATTER TO TILES

Place the six ceramic tiles on newspaper to protect surrounding areas. Use disposable surgical or rubber gloves to protect your hands while spattering. Spatter the mid-green porcelain paint mixture over the tiles by pushing a forefinger up through the bristles of the stencil brush. Repeat this process until the tiles are lightly and evenly covered with finely speckled colour.

Using separate stencil brushes, spatter with the olive green and white porcelain paint mixture until the tiles have the effect of being covered with a fine veil of pale green. Cover the palette with clingfilm and leave the tiles to dry.

3 POSITIVE AND NEGATIVE LEAF MOTIFS

Now spatter the positive and negative motifs onto the tiles – you will need three of each. Apply repositionable spray adhesive to the reverse of the positive and negative stencils and stick to the centre of the tiles.

Add the gold porcelain paint to the palette and dilute with porcelain paint thinner. Spatter inside the positive stencil and outside the negative stencil with the mid-green, olive green, white and gold porcelain paint mixtures until a subtle depth of colour has been created. Remove the stencil motifs and repeat the process on the remaining tiles. Cover the palette with clingfilm and leave the tiles to dry.

4 ADDING LEAF VEINS

Spray repositionable adhesive onto the reverse of the leaf-vein stencil and stick inside the positive and negative spattered leaf motifs. Use a piece of high-density foam to stencil some undiluted gold porcelain paint onto the leaf veins. Mix some of the dark green porcelain paint with the porcelain paint thinner and spatter the dark green through the veins. Repeat the process until the veins have been applied to all six leaf images. Put the tiles aside to dry for 24 hours.

5 BAKING TILES

Place the tiles directly onto the oven shelf of a cold oven. Set the temperature to 150° C (300° F, Gas Mark 2) and bake the tiles for 35 minutes. Open the oven door and allow to cool before removing the tiles (follow the paint manufacturer's instructions, as these may vary for different brands).

6 SPATTERING THE MIRROR FRAME

Stick a line of low-tack masking tape around the outside rim of the mirror. Pour a little of the white, mid-green, olive green and gold stencil paints into a divided palette or onto a paper plate and dilute until the paint colours have the consistency of single cream. Lay the mirror frame on some newspaper and very lightly spatter all over with a little of the mid-green, olive green, white and gold colour mixtures to produce a subtle film of colour. Leave to dry for 30 minutes or use a hairdryer to speed up the process. To spatter the upper and lower bands of the mirror frame, mask off the central ivory section of the mirror with low-tack masking tape and use the mid-green, olive green, white and gold colours to spatter these sections.

7 POSITIONING AND SPATTERING BORDER STENCIL

Spray repositionable adhesive onto the reverse of the first-layer border stencil and stick onto the lower band of the mirror frame. Cover the rest of the frame with paper and use the same colours to spatter through the first-layer border stencil to create a row of positive leaf images. Spatter until you have built up a subtle depth of colour. Remove the stencil and repeat the process on the upper band of the mirror frame. Leave to dry for 30 minutes or use a hairdryer to speed up the process.

8 APPLYING LEAF VEINS TO MIRROR

Spray repositionable adhesive onto the reverse of the second-layer stencil. Position the leaf veins of this stencil inside the row of leaf shapes spattered onto the lower band of the mirror frame and secure well. Pour a little dark green stencil paint into the divided palette and dilute to the consistency of single cream. Add some more gold to the palette, but do not dilute. Using the high-density foam stencil the gold through the veins, and then carefully spatter some of the dark green through the stencil. Repeat the process on the upper band of the mirror frame. Remove the masking tape from the outer rim of the frame, and leave to dry out fully overnight.

9 FINISHING AND MOUNTING TILES

Varnish the mirror frame with two coats of acrylic matt varnish or acrylic eggshell varnish. Then use the ruler, spirit level and pencil to mark up the positioning of the tiles, just under the band of ivory you have painted on the wall. Apply waterproof tiling adhesive to the area where tiles are to be mounted and secure the tiles, following the manufacturer's instructions. When dry, carefully apply waterproof grout to finish the splashback area.

Aquas & greens variations

Leaf motifs in coloured rectangles

Contrasting greens and simple leaf motifs create this contemporary scheme. Prime and paint the wall in ivory matt emulsion. Mark up a block of nine rectangles measuring 23 × 29 cm (9" × 11½"). Mask with painting tape. Seal edges with varnish. Paint randomly with pale lime, peppermint and pale moss-coloured matt emulsions (refer to Relief shells on neutral squares, page 72). Seal with matt acrylic varnish. Stencil simple leaf motifs in rows across the rectangles using ivory and pale green paints. Apply a coat of varnish.

Mermaid and dolphins mural

This charming stencilled mural shows the pictorial effect that can be achieved using a two-layered mural stencil. Seal walls with acrylic matt varnish. Stick the first-layer stencil in position. Stencil water – white, blue, green; dolphins – pale grey, blue; mermaid – green, gold, ochre. Overprint with metallic stencil paints. Remove, and position second-layer stencil. Stencil water as before; add metallic emerald to mermaid's tail; gold, and brown onto the shells. Finish with two coats of acrylic eggshell varnish.

Fantasy serpentine marble floor

Create this fantasy floor over two coats of ivory matt emulsion paint. Seal with acrylic eggshell varnish. Make up glazes by adding rich green and charcoal paint to the glaze mixture (use clear glaze recipe, step 1, page 92, Calacatta marble). Stencil a pale green, mid-grey, and pale grey geometric border around the floor. Apply a mottled effect in glazes (refer to step 2, page 93, Calacatta marble). Add vein lines in charcoal. Create a taped grid. Paint the large squares pale green, the rectangles pale grey, and small squares mid-grey. Varnish. Add a mottled effect and veins. Remove tapes, and varnish.

Distressed plaster with metallic finish

This finish is good for covering imperfect wall surfaces. Prime with acrylic primer. Paint with one coat of pale aqua matt emulsion. Use viridian artist's acrylic to tint impasto enough for two coats. Apply first coat with a decorator's steel float in a textured effect. When dry, apply a second coat by spreading some thick patches of impasto over the surface. Allow patches of first coat to show through. Leave to dry. Varnish with acrylic metallic varnish.

Spiral stamp variations

The simple spiral stamp is shown here in two variations. Paint the wall with two coats of turquoise matt emulsion, seal with acrylic matt varnish and stamp with white stamp paint. Alternatively, base-paint with white semi-gloss, colourwash with aqua, seal with acrylic matt varnish, and stamp with copper metallic stamp paint. Apply colourwash with a decorator's sponge in large figure-of-eight movements. Soften with a hog-hair softener.

Naturals

Tones of off-white, ivory, cream and stone give a sense of calm and tranquillity and a return to order – perfect for bathrooms for people who live busy lives or who just want to surround themselves with natural elegance and beauty. Natural-coloured spaces feel light, airy, clean and easy to live with.

Colours that emulate the look of plaster, natural stone and marble create a cool modern, yet classic feel that can be dressed up to give a lived in, traditional look or dressed down for an uncluttered, minimalist effect.

This versatile range of colours, with its inherent subtle differences, provides a wealth of decorative options and can be interpreted in both cool and warm colourways. Tones of off-white, stone and taupe have a cool effect, whereas tints of cream, sand and honey-beige add warmth and comfort. Cool schemes are enhanced by silver and sleek, brushed chrome; warm schemes naturally lend themselves to a touch of gilt and mellow gold. Use texture to add contrast, extra warmth and interest.

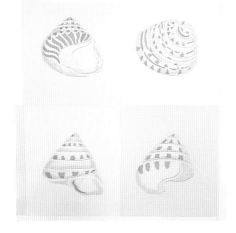

Subtle tone-on-tone neutral shades give this three-dimensional, shell-themed project a clean, contemporary and calming feel.

Relief shells on neutral squares

Five two-layered single-motif stencils are featured here. The possibilities for variation and experimentation with different combinations of the five designs are endless.

Where to apply

This effect can be used in different ways, either as a feature wall in one section of the room or repeating the squares throughout the room with the relief shells appearing only in specific places.

Difficulty level: moderate, but requiring patience.

YOU WILL NEED:

Two-layer shell stencils (pages 120 or 124) • white acrylic primer • ivory matt emulsion • three tones of cream matt emulsion • acrylic matt varnish • 250 ml/8 fl oz 3-D stencil paste or impasto • raw umber and yellow ochre universal tinter (or artist's acrylic or gouache) • painting tape • wide low-tack masking tape • decorator's brushes • decorator's steel float • palette knife • sanding block • repositionable spray adhesive • piece of high-density foam • fitch brush • small paint kettle • kitchen towel • spirit level • ruler • pencil • plastic rubber • tack cloth

PREPARATION

Prime and then paint the walls in the ivory matt emulsion, taking care to create as smooth a surface as possible. Varnish the walls with one coat of acrylic matt varnish.

NEUTRAL RECTANGLES

You will need three more neutral cream emulsion colours, each one varying in either hue or tone. Along with your base colour, these will form the four colours that will make up the painted rectangle base to the relief shells. For ease of reference label each emulsion paint *A, B, C* and *D* (*B* being the original ivory matt emulsion).

1 MARKING UP

Refer to Stencil Techniques (page 22). Use a spirit level, ruler and pencil to mark up a grid using small pencil marks for rectangles that are 23 × 18 cm (9" × 7"). You can vary these proportions to suit your room.

MASKING OFF *A* RECTANGLES

Stick lengths of painting tape or masking tape around the horizontal and vertical frame of the whole area. Use your pencil marks to guide you and to keep the tape straight. Then stick painting tape (or masking tape) vertically to the left and right of the columns designated as column 1 (see diagram below), which will create three columns 18 cm (7") wide. Now stick painting tape horizontally across these columns above and below your pencil marks to create the *A* rectangles. You will have now created six masked-off *A* rectangles ready to paint (see diagram below).

Layout of neutral rectangle colours

Column 1	Column 2	Column 1	Column 2	Column 1
B	C	B	C	B
A	D	A	D	A
B	C	B	C	B
A	D	A	D	A

PAINTING *A* RECTANGLES

The chart below gives the painting order. Use a fitch brush to apply acrylic matt varnish over the edges of the painting tape, to prevent bleeding. When this has dried paint the *A* rectangles with two coats of the cream matt emulsion that you have marked *A*. Remove the painting tape and allow the paint to dry.

Painting order		
A	Tape up and paint columns 1
B	Already painted
C	Tape up and paint columns 2
D	Tape up and paint columns 2

MASKING UP AND PAINTING *C* RECTANGLES

Once the paint is dry, stick painting tape or masking tape vertically to the left and right of the columns designated as column 2 (see diagram above), which will create two columns 18 cm (7") wide. Now stick painting tape horizontally across these columns above and below your pencil marks to create the *C* rectangles. You will now have created four masked-off *C* rectangles. Varnish the edges of the tape to prevent the paint bleeding. Allow to dry, and then paint with two coats of the emulsion you have marked as *C*. Leave the vertical strips of painting tape, but remove the tape stuck horizontally across the columns and allow the paint to dry.

MASKING UP AND PAINTING *D* RECTANGLES

Once the paint is dry, stick the painting tape or low-tack masking tape horizontally across the same columns, but above and below the pencil marks to create the *D* rectangles (see diagram above). Apply varnish to the tape edges, and, once dry, paint the rectangles you have marked as *D* with two coats of emulsion. Remove the tapes and allow to dry.

Once dry, rub off any visible pencil marks, brush, and then wipe down with a tack cloth. Varnish the area with one coat of acrylic matt varnish. Leave to dry for 24 hours so that the paint can fully harden.

6 RELIEF STENCILLING FIRST LAYER

Apply repositionable spray adhesive to the reverse of the first-layer stencils and stick to the centre of each of the rectangles on the bottom row of the grid. Mask off the edges of the stencils with painting tape or low-tack masking tape. Use a palette knife to scoop a tablespoon of 3-D stencil paste or impasto onto the right edge of a decorator's steel float and smooth over the first stencil. Apply more paste and repeat until each stencil is covered with a medium-thick, 3 mm (⅛") film of paste. Allow to dry and peel away the stencils very carefully.

7 STENCILLING UPPER ROWS

Use the palette knife to remove the excess paste from the stencils and restick them onto five of the rectangles on the two rows above. Apply the stencil paste as before. Allow to dry, and carefully peel away the stencils. Wash the stencils and allow the first layer of stencilling to dry overnight.

8 RELIEF STENCILLING THE SECOND LAYER

Add two drops of raw umber universal tinter (or artist's acrylic or gouache) to the remaining 3-D stencil paste and mix thoroughly. Take a sanding block and lightly sand the edges of the dry relief stencils. Apply repositionable spray adhesive to the reverse of the second layer of the five shell stencils and position on top of the first layer.

9 APPLYING TINTED PASTE

Use the decorator's steel float or a palette knife to apply the tinted stencil paste. Repeat on the remaining motifs. Remove the stencils and allow the paste to dry out fully. Sand any rough edges when dry.

10 ADDING EXTRA TONAL DEPTH

Add two drops of raw umber and yellow ochre tinters to a small cup of acrylic matt varnish and mix thoroughly. Dip a piece of high-density foam into the varnish and carefully wipe it around the raised outlines of the shell stencils. Use a damp cloth to wipe off any varnish that gets onto the surrounding areas. The finished shells will have a subtle, but definite three-dimensional effect.

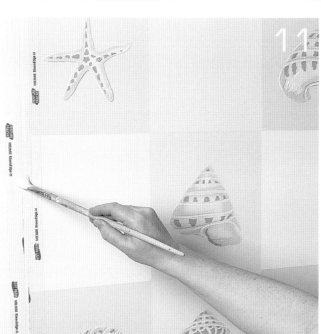

11 FINISHING

Use painting tape or low-tack masking tape to mask off a thin line running vertically down each edge of the rectangle grid and paint with the darkest cream matt emulsion tinted with a couple of drops of raw umber tinter. Allow to dry, remove the tape, and wipe down with a tack cloth. Varnish the whole panel with one coat of acrylic matt varnish.

This classic marble-effect bathroom brings a welcome decorative solution to the increasingly popular fashion for all things limestone in the bathroom, at a fraction of the cost.

Limestone marble Trompe L'Oeil

Although you cannot paint a Venetian marble bath, you can create your own marble walls and floors. These are complemented by an architecturally drawn, ageing Trompe L'Oeil mirror surround, which emulates the look of antique, moulded plasterwork or carved stone, and adds a touch of historical beauty.

Where to apply
The ornate surround can be applied straight to the wall around a piece of mirror glass. The marble effect is very effective when applied over moulded wood or plaster, as this emphasizes the natural lines and bands of the mineral deposits. Unsuitable for areas subject to high moisture.

Difficulty level: quite advanced, but the steps mean that anyone with enthusiasm can achieve good results.

PREPARATION
Use strong contact mirror glue to secure the mirror to the wall. Then cover the mirror with masking tape or paper to protect it. Marbled finishes need to be applied to very smooth surfaces, so take extra care in preparing the walls. Prime the walls with white acrylic primer, and then paint with two smooth coats of ivory matt emulsion.
Varnish with one coat of acrylic eggshell varnish.

YOU WILL NEED:

Mirror surround drawing (pages 121 or 124) • access to a photocopier • wooden molding or chair rail to fit your chosen area (optional) • medium-sized rectangular mirror • strong contact mirror glue • white acrylic primer • ivory matt emulsion • acrylic scumble glaze • acrylic eggshell varnish • raw umber, yellow ochre, sienna, white and black universal tinters or artist's acrylics • vermilion, cobalt, leaf-green, Vandyke brown, yellow ochre and white artist's gouaches or acrylics • decorator's brushes • hog-hair softener • badger softener • fitch brushes • artist's sable brushes and one-stroke brushes • soft varnishing brush (optional) • natural sea sponge • paint kettles • sealed containers • divided palette or paper plate • large sheets of 60 gsm tracing paper • drawing pencils • drawing fixative or hairspray • masking tape • protective paper • sanding block • spirit level • ruler • plastic rubber • tack cloth • cream cleaner

1 DESIGNING MIRROR SURROUNDS
Design your own drawing for the mirror surround or use the template drawing on page 121. Divide the drawing into three and enlarge to fit the width and length of the mirror, one section for below the mirror, and a section for the sides of the mirror. Enlarge each section to the right scale and lay tracing paper over the three copies. Secure with masking tape and trace with a drawing pencil.

2 TRANSFERRING THE FIRST HALF
Use a spirit level, ruler and pencil to make a few horizontal marks to line your tracings up to the sides of the mirror. Position the tracings and secure with masking tape. Trace over firmly with your pencil, using a ruler to draw over the straight lines. Now redraw over the pencil marks. Use drawing fixative or hairspray to fix the drawing and prevent smudging. Continue until one side of the mirror surround is complete.

3 TRACING SYMMETRICAL SECOND HALF

Flip the tracings over and carefully line up with the first half you have drawn, checking that the tracings are straight. Secure to the wall and repeat the tracing and drawing process; apply drawing fixative.

4 ADDING DEPTH TO DRAWING

Strengthen and thicken the pencil lines and shade some of the recessed areas to add more depth to the drawing. This will act as a guide when you come to paint in the details of this section.

Spray lightly with drawing fixative and remove any graphite smudges with a little cream cleaner on a damp cloth. Wipe away all traces of cleaner.

5 MIXING FIRST GLAZES

You will need a creamy-grey glaze and a buff, sandy glaze for the marble background. First make up approximately 1 litre (1¾ pints) of clear glaze using one-third of each of acrylic scumble glaze, acrylic eggshell varnish and water.

Pour about 100 ml (3½ fl oz) of this mixture into a sealed container and set aside for later, and then divide the remainder into two paint kettles. Tint these according to the following guidelines and mix thoroughly:

Creamy-grey glaze	Buff, sandy glaze
1 drop black tinter	4 drops yellow ochre tinter
6 drops white tinter	1 drop raw umber
1 tbsp (15 ml) ivory matt emulsion	2 drops burnt sienna
	1 tbsp (15 ml) ivory matt emulsion

Pour the buff, sandy glaze into a sealed container.

6 MOTTLING CREAMY-GREY GLAZE

Apply the glaze to the wall area to be marbled, and lightly over the drawn-out mirror surround. Wet the sea sponge and then squeeze out all water, until it is just damp. Apply the glaze in loose brushstrokes with a decorator's brush. Work a section at a time if marbling a large area. Dab over the glaze with the sea sponge to produce a soft, mottled effect, ensuring there is not too much of a build-up of glaze over the drawn areas. Leave for 20 minutes, or until dry.

7 MOTTLING BUFF, SANDY GLAZE

Rinse out the sea sponge and squeeze out the excess water. Apply the buff, sandy glaze in the same way as the first glaze. The whole area will now be covered in the mottled stage of the limestone effect. Allow to dry.

8 PREPARING GLAZES FOR MARBLE DRIFTS

Make a glaze roughly two tones darker than the original buff, sandy glaze by mixing 4 drops yellow ochre, 2 drops burnt sienna and 1 drop raw umber tinter into the clear glaze in the sealed container.

Make a translucent, soft-ivory glaze by mixing 10 ml (2 tsp) of ivory matt emulsion with 10 ml (2 tsp) of acrylic scumble glaze, and a little of the original creamy-grey glaze. Cover the glazes until needed. Also have the original buff, sandy glaze ready.

9 BUFF DRIFTS

The drifts of mineral deposits in the marble are now applied. These are usually large tapering bands of colour starting wide at the top and tapering down to a thinner line. To achieve a realistic effect, keep the number of drifts to a minimum. Add to the overall Trompe L'Oeil realism by working the colour over the moulded section around the mirror as well as any wooden moulding. Working on one drift at a time, use a wide fitch to paint loose wavering bands of sandy buff glaze across the marbled area. Very lightly soften these with a hog-hair softener. Then while the glaze is still a little wet, brush over the lower or upper edge of each drift repeatedly in one direction, until subtle ridges or tidemarks start to appear.

10 DARKER BUFF EDGES AND TRANSLUCENT IVORY

Use a small fitch brush dipped in the darker buff glaze to loosely paint irregular lines on one edge of the marble drifts. Work one area at a time. Soften first with the hog-hair softener and then very lightly sweep the badger softener back and forth over the area to make the line look as if it is 'sitting' in the glaze.

Add uneven bands of ivory above each drift and soften as before. Continue working in this way until you have built up the drift effect across the wall.

12 TROMPE L'OEIL DIMENSIONS

Use the Vandyke brown, yellow ochre, and white gouache or acrylics to mix up a mocha brown, a pale buff brown and an ivory colour. Add a little of the original glazes to these three colours to give them a better flow for painting and to make them tone in with the rest of the scheme. Use these colours to gradually build up the three-dimensional effect of the mirror surround by adding highlights and shadows to the different moulded aspects of the underlying drawing.

11 SMALL FRESCO-LIKE FRIEZE

In a divided palette, mix some of the buff, sandy glaze with the vermilion, cobalt and leaf-green gouache or acrylic to make three soft muddy tones. Use an artist's sable brush to paint these tones onto the flowers and leaves on the small frieze under the mirror. Work one section at a time applying the paint with the artist's sable brush and softening it with a hog-hair softener or soft varnishing brush. Gradually build up these colours, also using the darker buff glaze to paint in areas around the flowers.

13 FINISHING

Add any final details or added depth. Then mix a drop each of raw umber, yellow ochre, and burnt sienna tinters with 250 ml (8 fl oz) acrylic eggshell varnish, and varnish the whole area. Add a coat of clear eggshell varnish. Carefully peel away the masking tape and clean off any paint marks.

Naturals variations

Faux stucco squares and plaster mirror

Warm honey tones of classic polished plaster look beautiful. Prime and paint the walls with two coats of ivory matt emulsion. Cover with a taped grid at 30 cm (12") intervals. Lightly varnish with acrylic eggshell varnish. Apply a coat of light beige matt emulsion in loose criss-cross strokes. Mix a warm-beige glaze (use buff glaze recipe from Limestone marble Trompe L'Oeil, step 5, page 77). Apply to each square and stipple lightly. Add two drops of burnt sienna tinter and a little water to the glaze. Repeat the stippling process. Remove the tape. Paint a fine shadow line down and across one side of the grout lines in mocha brown. Varnish with acrylic gloss varnish. To make the mirror, stick 2 mm (1⁄16") mirror glass onto a piece of 12 mm (1⁄2") MDF. Mask off mirror then apply beige-tinted impasto. Varnish with one coat of acrylic matt varnish.

Pale gold damask

Here ivory and gold give subtle, reflective highlights. Prime and paint the wall with two coats of ivory matt emulsion and varnish with two coats of acrylic matt varnish. Stencil the first layer of the damask stencil on your chosen wall area, first in cream and then over-printed with pale gold stencil paint. Then apply the second-layer stencil in a creamy ochre (refer to Damask walls, step 4, page 42).

Travertine marble effect and decorative border

Create this cool floor for a sense of luxury. Prime and paint with two coats of ivory matt emulsion. Seal with acrylic eggshell varnish. Make guide marks for the border stencil. Create a taped grid inside them. Add tape for small diamond shapes at the joins of the squares, and triangles where the tiles meet the border. Mix a pale grey and buff-coloured glaze (use recipe from Limestone marble Trompe L'Oeil, step 5, page 77). Apply a mot-tled effect over the whole floor and soften. Make up an ivory and a darker buff glaze (step 8, page 78). Apply soft stripes on the large squares. Stencil the border with the ivory paint. Remove tapes. Paint fine edges to the border and grout lines. Varnish.

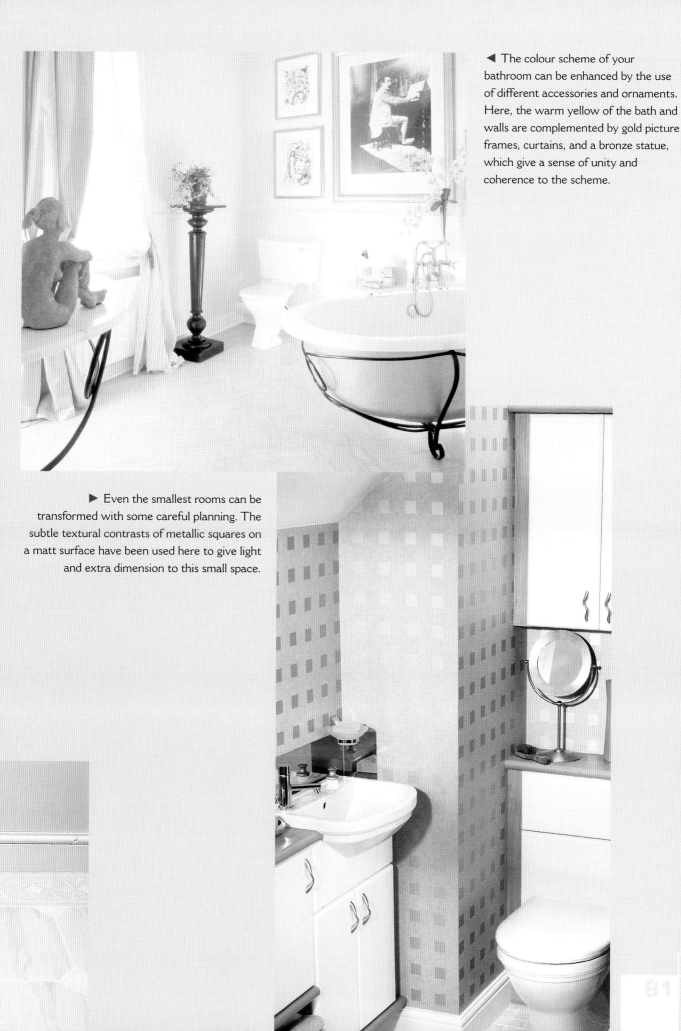

◀ The colour scheme of your bathroom can be enhanced by the use of different accessories and ornaments. Here, the warm yellow of the bath and walls are complemented by gold picture frames, curtains, and a bronze statue, which give a sense of unity and coherence to the scheme.

▶ Even the smallest rooms can be transformed with some careful planning. The subtle textural contrasts of metallic squares on a matt surface have been used here to give light and extra dimension to this small space.

White to Grey

The white-to-grey palette gives both subtle and striking monochromatic possibilities with surprising versatility in style and effect, achieved by altering the proportions of white and shades of grey.

A predominantly white scheme will produce a clean, reflective, airy space, which stands in its own right or acts as a perfect backdrop for accents of contrasting or toning colours. A scheme comprising several tints of pale gray will create a light, yet truly neutral, restful feel. Combine pure white and grey tones for a contemporary look – ideal for abstract or geometric styles – or soften the palette by using pale ivory and blue-greys or green-greys for more traditional decorative schemes.

Use predominantly paler tints with accents of darker greys and charcoal to create a sophisticated scheme with lively contrasts and tonal variations; or try equal proportions of white and dark charcoal for highly contrasting, striking schemes that introduce a sense of formal elegance – particularly effective for stylish floors; silver metallic accents work extremely well with this palette.

Create the light, airy style of the northeastern seaboard of the Atlantic in this New England themed bathroom.

New England style

Here the look is a blend of old-world charm and relaxed, contemporary living with a fresh, clean feel. Cool neutral whites and palest greys form the basis of the colour scheme for wood panelling, painted walls, bathroom furniture, a bleached wood mirror frame, and a monochromatic shoreline border, given extra definition with navy-grey check fabrics.

Where to apply

The walls here are a combination of painted flat walls and tongue-and-groove wooden panelling. Vary the proportions of panelling and painted walls to suit your bathroom, or cover all walls with either effect.

Difficulty level: **moderate.**

> ## Note
> Refer to page 40 for advice on constructing tongue-and-groove panelling.

Painted tongue-and-groove

New England is renowned for its wooden panelling painted in whites and light colours; here a subtle pale grey tone is used for this simple style of panelling.

PREPARATION

This project uses 10 cm (4") V-joint tongue-and-groove panelling known as TGV. Once the wood panelling has been constructed, fill and sand any nail holes or cracks in the wood (refer to Damask Walls, page 40). Remove dust with a dusting brush. Apply knotting solution with a fitch brush to all visible knots, to prevent any discolouration from resin. Clean the brush with methylated spirits immediately after use.

> ### YOU WILL NEED:
>
> 10 cm (4") V-joint tongue-and-groove timber (TGV) to cover the area to be panelled • wood filler • knotting solution • methylated spirits • white acrylic primer • very pale grey matt emulsion • acrylic matt varnish • decorator's brushes • fitch brush • palette knife • sanding block • dusting brush

PAINTING

Prime the wood with one coat of white acrylic primer. Make sure that you push the primer into the V joins to achieve full coverage. Apply two coats of very pale grey matt emulsion to the panelled walls, allowing plenty of time between coats for the paint to dry out in the V joins. When the paint has fully dried apply two coats of acrylic matt varnish.

Shoreline Border

The soft grey theme is continued on the walls, with the addition of a band of ivory for the border stencil. The shoreline stencil is applied in a monochromatic palette, which creates a tonal, three-dimensional effect.

PREPARATION

Prime the walls with a coat of white acrylic primer and then paint with two coats of pale grey matt emulsion.

YOU WILL NEED:

Shoreline border stencil (pages 121 or 124) • pale grey matt emulsion • ivory matt emulsion • white acrylic primer • acrylic matt varnish • stencil paints in ivory, pale grey, blue-grey and dark blue-grey • repositionable spray adhesive • divided palette or paper plate • high-density foam in 4 cm (1½") squares • kitchen towel • painting tape • masking tape • paint kettle • spirit level • ruler • pencil • plastic rubber • permanent marker • hairdryer (if necessary) • tack cloth

MARKING UP STENCIL

Refer to Stencil Techniques (page 22). Draw a horizontal line onto the first layer of the shoreline border stencil 1 cm (½") below the lower edge of the design. Then lay the second-layer stencil over the first, line up the motifs in the design, and trace the horizontal line. If the stencil does not have registration dots, check the motifs are still lined up and cut registration dots in the corners.

1 PAINTING BAND

To paint a band of ivory matt emulsion across the wall, make guide marks 24 cm (9½") apart for the border. Stick painting tape along the marks, and seal with varnish.

Mix 1 tbsp (15 ml) of pale grey matt emulsion with 500 ml (17½ fl oz) of ivory matt emulsion and apply two coats to the band. Remove the top length of tape.

Stick painting tape 5 mm (¼") above the lower tape, to make a thin line. Seal with varnish and paint with the blue-grey stencil paint. Remove the tapes and allow to dry. Varnish the walls with one coat of acrylic matt varnish.

3 ADDING DEPTH OF COLOUR

Apply dark blue-grey paint to the tail feathers of the seagull on the highest post and all of the birds' beaks. Add highlights to the birds with ivory stencil paint. Make light pencil marks through the registration holes to position the next layer.

2 POSITIONING AND STENCILLING FIRST LAYER OF BORDER

Spray repositionable adhesive onto the reverse of the stencil and secure to the wall. Pour some of the ivory, pale grey, blue-grey and dark blue-grey stencil paints into a divided palette or onto a paper plate.

Use the pale grey lightly over the whole stencil, and then go back, overprinting the lower parts of the birds' bodies and the water. Use the blue-grey stencil paint to add more depth to some of the water, the wooden posts, the lower parts of the birds' bodies, and the tail feathers.

4 REMAINING REPEATS

Remove the stencil and reposition to the right of the first motif. Repeat the stencilling process. Refer back to the section you have just stencilled to maintain the colour sequence.

5 STENCILLING SECOND LAYER OF BORDER

Spray repositionable adhesive onto the reverse of the second-layer stencil and position over the first layer, lining up the registration dots.

Use the blue-grey for the upper wing feathers and some details on the posts. Use the dark blue-grey for the remainder of the posts, the wings and feathers, and to add depth to the beaks.

When the border is complete, varnish with two coats of acrylic matt varnish.

Cabinet and Mirror Frame

The painted wood theme is continued with a tongue-and-groove cabinet – painted in ivory and lightly distressed – and a rough timber frame, which is given a bleached, driftwood effect.

YOU WILL NEED:

Pine cabinet or other piece of furniture • rough pine frame and mirror glass • white acrylic primer • ivory wood paint or matt emulsion • acrylic matt varnish • knotting solution • methylated spirits • decorator's brushes • fitch brush • sanding block • medium-grade sandpaper • masking tape • cotton • lint-free cloth • perspex, or safe, shatterproof glass

PREPARATION

Refer to the guidelines in Preparation (page 14) for your particular cabinet. Sand the painted or bare surfaces thoroughly with medium-grade sandpaper to create a key. Apply knotting solution to any visible knots on bare or new wood to prevent any discolouration from resin. Cover any exposed hinges with masking tape.

1 PAINTING AND DISTRESSING THE CABINET

Apply one coat of white acrylic primer, making sure that paint is pushed into all the tongue-and-groove joins. Once the primer is dry, paint the cabinet with two coats of ivory wood paint, or ivory matt emulsion.

When the paint has completely dried use a piece of medium-grade sandpaper to distress the edges of the cabinet and cabinet doors. This will create a subtle distressed effect. Take care not to overdo this – keep the sanding minimal.

Finally, varnish with two coats of acrylic matt varnish. To add a finishing touch, apply the same treatment to the cabinet knobs.

For cabinets supporting sinks, protect the top with a sheet of shatterproof glass. Holes for sink plumbing should be made in cabinets supporting basin or bowl sinks before decorating. Use shatterproof glass to protect cabinets (a glazier should be able to cut out holes for plumbing).

2 BLEACHED EFFECT TO FRAME

Sand any rough edges off the frame and remove dust with a brush. Working on one side of the frame at a time, brush on the ivory wood paint or matt emulsion and wipe off immediately with a slightly damp cotton cloth, so that the paint stays in the grain, but is wiped away from the raised areas. Repeat on the three remaining sides of the frame. To make the effect more dramatic, repeat the process once the first coat of paint has dried.

This geometric repeat stencil creates a cool and stylish backdrop for modern fixtures and fittings, as well as mirrors and chrome accessories.

Geometric repeat

This design features a simple two-layer stencil. The grey and silver on white colour scheme and bold shape of the stencil gives a really sleek, contemporary look.

Where to apply
Use on one wall or as an all-over wallpaper effect for the whole room.

Difficulty level: **easy, as the design works on a square repeat basis.**

YOU WILL NEED:

Two-layer geometric repeat stencil (pages 117 or 124) • white acrylic primer • soft white matt emulsion • acrylic matt varnish • acrylic eggshell varnish • stencil paints in pale grey, silver and charcoal grey • decorator's brushes • repositionable spray adhesive • palette or paper knife • high-density foam in 4 cm (1½") squares • kitchen towel • spirit level • ruler • set square • pencil • permanent marker • plastic rubber • tack cloth • hairdryer (if necessary)

PREPARATION
Prime and then paint the walls in soft white matt emulsion, taking care to create as smooth a surface as possible. Varnish the walls with one coat of acrylic matt varnish.

1 MARKING UP
Refer to Stencil Techniques (page 22). Use a spirit level, ruler and pencil to mark up horizontal registration guides at the top of the wall and to make vertical marks at the left edge of the wall. These marks will be important registration guides to keep the geometric design square while you are printing. Draw corresponding horizontal and vertical lines onto the stencil using a set square and permanent marker.

2 POSITIONING THE STENCIL

Apply repositionable spray adhesive to the reverse of the first layer of the stencil and secure the stencil in the top left-hand corner of the wall for the first repeat, lining up the horizontal and left-hand vertical registration guides. Ensure the cut-out shapes are fully stuck to the wall to prevent bleeding. Refer to Stencil Techniques (page 22).

3 STENCILLING THE FIRST REPEAT

Pour some of the pale grey stencil paint onto a palette or paper plate and apply using a piece of high-density foam. Stencil in light sweeping movements working in the vertical and horizontal direction of the design. Work from the top left-hand corner of the stencil to the bottom right-hand corner. If any patches of the stencil look a little transparent, overprint them with the same colour to build up opacity. When the grey has dried, overprint the stencil using the silver stencil paint to give the first layer a metallic lustre. Carefully peel the stencil away from the wall.

4 STENCILLING THE SECOND REPEAT AND FIRST LINE

When the first repeat is dry (use a hairdryer if you want to speed the process up) position the stencil to the right of the first repeat. Make sure that the horizontal line at the top of the stencil lines up with the horizontal marks at the top of the wall, as well as positioning the left-hand side of the stencil so that the gap between the already printed motif and the new repeat is the same as in the design itself. In this way the design will have a continuous effect. Repeat the stencilling process using the pale grey and silver colours, moving to the right across the top of the wall, until the first horizontal row is complete.

5 COMPLETING THE FIRST LAYER

When the first line is complete, place the stencil under the first repeat, on the left-hand side. Ensure that the line on the left-hand side of the stencil lines up with the registration marks on the left-hand side of the wall, at the same time as positioning the top of the stencil so that the gap between the already printed motif and the new repeat is the same as in the design itself.

Stencil this repeat and then continue working from left to right until this row is complete as before. Continue this process until the first layer covers the whole of the area to be stencilled.

6 STENCILLING THE SECOND LAYER

As soon as the first few repeats of the first layer are complete and dry, you can start working on the second layer in the top left-hand corner. This means that you can be working on both layers at the same time, and can move from one to the other while the stencil paint is drying.

Apply repositionable spray adhesive to the reverse of the second-layer stencil. Position the stencil by lining it up so that the smaller lines fit within the shapes of the first layer and do not overlap into any of the gaps. Stick the stencil securely to the wall to prevent any bleeding.

Stencil first with the charcoal grey stencil paint and when this is dry, go over it with the silver stencil paint.

7 REMOVING THE STENCIL

When you peel the stencil away, you will see that the second layer gives a pewter effect on top of the paler silver.

8 COMPLETING THE SECOND LAYER

Continue this process over all of the first-layer stencil motifs until all of the geometric shapes have the metallic ridged shape inside them. If you are stencilling a large area, you may find that the smaller cut-out shapes in the second layer will become clogged with paint. If this is the case, remove the stencil and wash off the build-up of paint, dry the stencil and then continue printing.

9 FINISHING

Rub off any visible pencil marks and brush off any loose bits of rubber and then wipe over the whole surface using a tack cloth to ensure the surface is dust free. Finally varnish with two coats of acrylic eggshell varnish.

White-grey polished marble has a timeless elegance and appeal. This wide, drift-veined version gives walls a cool chic complemented by the graphic floor.

Calacatta marble

Calacatta marble has a depth that appears both striking and subtle, as the carbon mineral deposits embedded in its surface change to reveal tones that range from sharp contrasts to amorphous opacity. The effective use of a monochromatic palette – from white to translucent charcoal – and different glazes make it possible to recreate this effect.

Where to apply

The Calacatta marble is best applied in panels on walls or pillars, or you can mark off areas of wall on which to apply the finish. The floor is designed as an all-over floor treatment. Wall and floor finishes can be used in their own right or together as a complementary scheme. Walls should be as smooth as possible to look realistic, and the floor finish is most effective applied to a flat surface, such as MDF or hardboard, which is probably best laid by a professional. However, if you are enthusiastic about DIY, refer to a comprehensive DIY manual to guide you through the relevant stages. You will need to work with sheets of 4 mm (⅛") or 6 mm (¼") thick MDF or hardboard.

Difficulty level: this is quite advanced, but by following the steps carefully it will be possible for anyone with enthusiasm to achieve success.

YOU WILL NEED:

White acrylic primer • white matt emulsion • acrylic scumble glaze • acrylic eggshell varnish • acrylic eggshell floor varnish • black, raw umber, white and yellow ochre universal tinter or artist's acrylics • 60 ml (2 fl oz) sample pot black matt emulsion • wood filler • sealant • decorator's brushes • fitch brushes (medium and small) • hog-hair softener • badger softener • paint kettles • three sealed containers or jars with lids • lint-free household cloth • kitchen towel • 7 mm (¼") lining tape • painting tape • sanding block • spirit level • set square • ruler • pencil • scissors • tack cloth • clingfilm

Calacatta Walls

PREPARATION

Marbled finishes need to be applied to very smooth surfaces to make them realistic, so take extra care in preparing the walls. Prime and then paint the walls with two smooth coats of white matt emulsion, sanding between coats. Varnish with one coat of acrylic eggshell varnish. Ideally allow the paint to cure and the varnish to harden for 48 hours. Mask off any areas not to be marbled with painting tape, and seal with varnish along the tape edges.

1 MIXING GLAZES

You will need a pale grey, a mid-grey, and a charcoal grey glaze for the marble finishes.

First make up approximately 1 litre (1¾ pints) of clear glaze using one-third each of acrylic scumble glaze, acrylic eggshell varnish and water. Pour half of this mixture into a paint kettle and divide the other half between two paint kettles. Tint the divided glazes according to the following guidelines:

Glaze 1: pale grey 500 ml (17 fl oz)	Glaze 2: mid-grey 250 ml (8 fl oz)	Glaze 3: charcoal grey 250 ml (8 fl oz)
2 drops black tinter	3 drops black tinter	6 drops black tinter
3 drops raw umber	3 drops raw umber	2 drops white
		3 drops raw umber
Pour the mid-grey and charcoal grey glazes into sealed containers.		

2 APPLYING MOTTLED PALE GREY

Use a decorator's brush to brush the pale grey glaze loosely over the first section of the wall or walls to be marbled. Work in areas of up to 2 m (6½'), which will allow you to do everything you need to do within the 'open time' of the glaze mixture.

Dampen the household cloth, scrunch it up into a loose ball and dab over the surface of the glaze creating a mottled pattern. Rescrunch the cloth frequently to create different shapes within the mottled effect.

3 SOFTENING GLAZE

Go back to the point where you started, and lightly soften with the hog-hair softener by passing the brush over the glaze in light criss-cross movements. While the glaze is still a little wet, go back to the start and brush the hog-hair softener repeatedly over the same patch in one direction, until subtle ridges or tidemarks start to appear. Repeat process in sections across the wall to create the soft, mottled background for the marble. Clean the softener in soapy water, rinse and shake out well. Allow the glaze to dry for 30 minutes or until touch dry.

4 SOFT WIDE DRIFTS AND AMOEBIC SHAPES

Establish the directional flow of the marble drifts. Use a fitch brush dipped in the same pale grey glaze to loosely paint wide, broken, diagonal channels across the area. Soften these in the same way using the hog-hair softener. Then, picking up on the patterns made within the glaze, loosely paint and soften amoebic (elongated irregular cell) shapes of different proportions into some of the drift shapes.

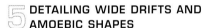

5 DETAILING WIDE DRIFTS AND AMOEBIC SHAPES

Use the mid-grey glaze on a small fitch brush to loosely paint a smudgy line on one edge of some parts of the soft, wide veins and the amoebic shapes. Work one area at a time. Soften first with the hog-hair softener and then very lightly sweep the badger softener back and forth over the area to make the line look as if it is 'sitting' in the glaze.

Mottled Marble Checkerboard Floor

PREPARATION

On MDF or hardboard floors, fill any holes made by tack heads with a wood filler and use an appropriate sealant to fill the sheeting joins. Ensure all surfaces are smooth and completely dust free. Prime and then paint with two smooth coats of white flat matt emulsion, sanding between coats.

1 CALACATTA BORDER TO FLOOR

Use the set square, ruler and pencil to make a series of registration marks 18 cm (7") in from the edge of the floor. Stick painting tape along these marks. Seal the edge of the tape with varnish.

Marble the border in the Calacatta style following steps 1–6 for marbling the walls. Allow to dry and remove the tapes.

6 CHARCOAL EDGING

Use the charcoal grey glaze on a small fitch to paint some thin, smudgy lines on the edges of some of the wide veins, and build up the contrast and intensity around the amoebic shapes. Then soften with the hog-hair and the badger softeners as before.

2 TAPING UP THE TILE GRID

Use the 7 mm (¼") lining tape to create the effect of grout lines. Stick the tape around the inner edge of the border. Then measure 40½ cm (16") from the outside edge of two adjacent lines across the floor. Stick the tape on the outer edge of these marks to ensure the correct dimension; if the square is less than 40½ cm (16"), the tape has been stuck on the wrong side of the line.

Mark up and stick down tape for the next two adjacent lines, measuring 40½ cm (16") from outside edge of last tape. Continue this process to build up a tiled grid. The last square may be cut short, but this will look quite natural, as the same thing would happen on a real floor. Seal tape with varnish to prevent bleeding.

3 MOTTLED MARBLE EFFECT

Starting furthest from the door, mask off the border with painting tape and seal with varnish. Then use the same technique to apply, mottle and soften the pale grey glaze from the Calacatta marble glazes to the whole floor area inside the masked-off border, working straight over the tape grid.

When dry, apply another layer of the pale glaze in the same way as the first. Allow to dry.

Tip

It is always best to start work on floors at the point furthest from the door and work towards the door.

4 CHEQUERBOARD EFFECT

The chequerboard effect is achieved by applying a dark charcoal glaze to alternate squares. Use the lining-tape grid as a guide to mask off alternate squares, with the first dark charcoal square being in the corner that meets the marbled walls. Cut lengths of painting tape to mask off squares, trimming the ends.

Mix 200 ml (7 fl oz) acrylic scumble glaze with the pot of black matt emulsion. Add three drops of raw umber tinter, two drops of yellow ochre tinter and equal amounts of acrylic eggshell varnish and water until the consistency is one of thick cream. Mix thoroughly.

5 APPLYING DARK GLAZE

The technique for applying this glaze is the same as for the pale glaze. Apply a second layer of this to create the depth of the dark charcoal. Dab a piece of scrunched-up clingfilm to create a few lighter mottled patches.

6 LIGHT VEINS

Mix some acrylic scumble glaze, white matt emulsion and a little pale grey glaze together to make a soft, translucent white.

Use a small fitch brush to paint small, random veins onto the dark charcoal and soften with the hog-hair softener. Vary the position of these veins square to square to create a realistic effect.

7 REMOVING TAPES AND FINISHING

Allow to dry for 20 minutes, and then carefully remove the painting tape and tape grid to reveal clear grout lines. Allow to dry thoroughly for at least 24 hours. Wipe over with a tack cloth, and varnish with two coats of acrylic eggshell floor varnish. Do not use for 48 hours.

White to grey variations

Shoreline mirror

This beautiful mirror frame is ideal for a sea-themed bathroom. Drill eight 21 cm (¼") holes around the edge of 12 mm (½") thick MDF measuring 38 × 45 cm (15" × 18"). Prime. Stick 2 mm (⅟₁₆")thick mirror glass measuring 14 × 18 cm (5 ½" × 7") onto the fibreboard. Mask off the glass. Paint the frame with pale grey matt emulsion. Paint several flat shells with white acrylic primer. Stick to the bottom of the frame, using tile adhesive. Stipple 3-D stencil paste or impasto around the shells. Remove tape. Stick 7 mm (¼") soft white rope around the mirror with adhesive and seal edges with PVA. Thread a 2 m (6½') length of the rope through the holes in the mirror. Tie double knots in the rope and seal ends with PVA.

Abstract Oriental calligraphy on raised squares

Use this design to create an elegant and striking feature wall. Prepare, prime and paint three 30 cm (12") squares of 12 mm (½") MDF and the walls with two coats of soft white matt emulsion. Seal wall and squares with acrylic matt varnish. Stick torn painting tape (refer to Soft vertical stripes, step 3, page 44) in a steep diagonal line on the wall, then onto the squares. Seal tape with varnish. Loosely paint and stipple a pale grey glaze (see Calacatta marble, step 1, page 92) to the right of the tape. Stencil oriental motifs onto the squares in pale grey and charcoal. Overprint with pearl and silver stencil paints.

Koi carp etched glass

Create this beautiful, subtle etched-effect on glass – use on windows, mirrors and the outside of shower screens or door panels. This is not a fully permanent finish. Clean the glass surface to be decorated with methylated spirits. Stick your stencil securely onto the glass. Ensure good ventilation and spray several even coats of etching/frosting spray onto the glass. Leave for an hour, then carefully peel away the stencil (refer to Etched glass squares, step 5, page 53). Allow to dry fully.

▶ Marbling has been used on the side of this bath to give this neutral scheme extra interest and a look that is individual and classically elegant.

◀ The structured graphic effect of this bathroom is achieved by the simple, but well considered use of black and white, with additional metallic greys and marble textures. The strong lines of the chrome towel rail further emphasize this stylish statement.

Colour Combos

The fascination with combining different colours in decorative schemes has been a strong influence throughout design history. Well-known principles of combining include polychromatic, harmonious, contrasting and complementary schemes based on either synchronizing or contrasting colour combinations (see Colour, pages 24–25).

Whether following established principles or simply working from instinct, colour combining opens the door to a wonderful world of rich choices and diverse decorative possibilities. Further creative dimensions open up either by choosing pastel tints, bright colours or deep shades; or by combining different colour intensities and shades together. Try a palette that has two or three main colours, or else a scheme that has a predominant background colour with added accents.

Pastel combinations produce a light, yet crisp feel, as seen in the striped shower curtain project which has both harmonizing and contrasting elements; whereas bright polychromatic schemes give a lively, warm atmosphere, as shown in the Mediterranean bathroom, using primary colours, typical of that region. The Indian style bathroom shows the richness of eastern influences in a predominantly one-coloured palette with bright, contrasting accents.

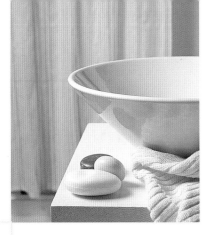

These beautiful, soft-pastel stripes on pure white cotton voile have a clean, simple and very modern feel, with a soft touch.

Striped shower curtain

This is used as an outer shower curtain to give a light, diaphanous, and airy feel to the bathroom.

Where to apply

This outer shower curtain is designed to be used with a waterproof shower curtain, which should be hung behind it. This treatment would look equally beautiful hung at the bathroom window, allowing the light to stream through.

Difficulty level: **this is a simple project, but the taping up and colour sequence can be a little confusing at first.**

PREPARATION

To make up the shower curtain, first measure the area it will cover. If you are able to buy extra-wide fabric, simply add on 20 cm (8") for hems at the top and bottom. If the fabric is too narrow buy enough for two lengths plus 40 cm (16") for hems. If you are working with two lengths of narrow fabric, sew the seam of the curtain and then cut the width to size allowing 10 cm (4") for the side hems. Pin a double 2½ cm (1") turning at the side edge and a double 2½ cm (1") hem along the bottom. Machine-sew and press. Pin a double 7½ cm (3") turning along the top edge. Machine-sew and press.

100% cotton voile or cotton lawn in white to fit your shower curtain (usual dimensions 183 × 183 cm (72" × 72") • large tabletop or counter • fabric stencil paints in pale creamy-green, pale turquoise-blue, light green and pale sugar-pink • dressmaker's pins • sewing machine • sewing thread • low-tack masking tape in 5 cm (2"), 2½ cm (1"), and 7 mm (¼") widths • high-density foam in 4 cm (1½") squares • sheet of bubble wrap • lining paper • divided palette or paper plate • kitchen towel • plastic bag or sheet of acetate • pencil • 15 cm (6") plastic ruler • small strip of cardboard for marking up • scissors • fixings for hanging curtain (see Finishing, step 9)

1 STICKING FABRIC TO TABLE

Cover a large tabletop with the sheet of bubble wrap then with lining paper, and secure with masking tape. Use the ruler and pencil to draw a 14 mm (½") line horizontally across the edge of the lining paper. Line up the side edge of the curtain with the line you have drawn and stick the fabric down so that the masking tape is exactly half on the table and half on the fabric. This will create a clean edge to the striped curtain.

2 TAPING WIDE AND NARROW STRIPES

Start by measuring 2½ cm (1") from the edge of the masking tape, making small pencil marks at intervals down the length of the fabric.

Carefully stick a line of 2½ cm (1") low-tack masking tape along the outer side of the marks you have made. Don't worry if it wrinkles a little. As long as the tape is securely stuck down, the end result will still be a straight line. Trim the edge of the tape so that it finishes right at the end of the fabric and does not stick onto the table.

To create the two thin stripes, measure 14 mm (½") from the edge of this tape and make pencil marks at intervals as before and then stick down a line of 14 mm (½") low-tack masking tape.

Measure a further 14 mm (½") and stick down another line of 5 cm (2") low-tack masking tape. Repeat the wide and narrow stripes until you have taped up the whole curtain.

Refer to the diagram below to help with the tape measuring.

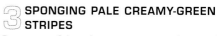

stripe space	tape	stripe space	tape	stripe space	tape	stripe space
1" (2½ cm)	5 cm (2")	14 mm (½")	14 mm (½")	14 mm (½")	5 cm (2")	1" (2½ cm)

Tape layout

3 SPONGING PALE CREAMY-GREEN STRIPES

Pour some of the pale creamy-green, pale turquoise-blue, and light green fabric stencil paints into a divided palette. Dip a piece of high-density foam into the pale creamy-green fabric paint and dab off the excess on the kitchen towel. Wipe the pale creamy-green on the sponge over the first 2½ cm (1") stripe space to create the first pale creamy-green stripe.

4 SPONGING PALE TURQUOISE-BLUE STRIPES

Dip another piece of high-density foam into the pale turquoise-blue fabric stencil paint and dab off the excess on the kitchen towel. Wipe the pale turquoise-blue on the sponge over the two thin 14 mm (½") stripe spaces to create the first thin, pale turquoise-blue stripes.

5 SPONGING LIGHT GREEN STRIPES

Now sponge the light green onto the next 2½ cm (1") stripe space to create a light green stripe. Once you have sponged in all of the stripes across the curtain, carefully peel back all of the tapes and discard. Allow the curtain to dry for up to an hour.

6 COLOUR ORDER

The order that the colours are applied onto the curtain has been devised so that it takes four repeats of the stripes with the same colours, for example with the pale turquoise-blue to be used for the double stripes. This gives the curtain much more interest, as the colours on the different widths of stripes keeps changing. Keep working in colour order, regardless of the size of stripes and the colour repeat will happen automatically. The pink is not used at this stage. The colour order moving across the curtain is pale creamy-green, pale turquoise-blue, light green.

7 TAPING FOR SUGAR-PINK STRIPES

Cut a strip of cardboard exactly 5 cm (2") wide and draw two lines to make a 7 mm (¼") band in the centre of this cardboard. This will be used as a pattern to mark up the sugar-pink stripes.

The sugar-pink stripes are placed between the pale turquoise-blue and light green stripes. Place the marked-up cardboard between these stripes and make two marks on the fabric that correspond with the two lines on the cardboard. As before, mark up at intervals along the length of the fabric. Repeat this process between each of the pale turquoise-blue and light green stripes. Stick two lines of 2½ cm (1") low-tack masking tape along these marks to make up the 7 mm (¼") stripes.

8 SPONGING SUGAR-PINK STRIPES

Pour some of the pale sugar-pink fabric stencil paint into the divided palette. Dip a sponge into the fabric stencil paint, dab off the excess on kitchen towel, and sponge between the lines of masking tape.

9 FINISHING

Allow to dry for 10 minutes then remove the tapes. Lift the fabric off the table and hang to dry. Iron with a hot iron on the reverse side to fix the fabric stencil paints. To hang the finished striped curtain with your waterproof shower curtain, you can either use a eyelet kit to make shower-curtain holes in the top of the fabric, or sew thin strips of voile to make tie-top headings, or use no-sew curtain clips.

This themed project will allow you to bring the romantic and exotic opulence of India to your bathroom with rich, delicately patterned motifs, bright jewel-like coloured walls and rich gold accents.

Indian style bathroom

Follow these steps to create this exciting yet intimate look, for a space that will be perfect to unwind and wash away the cares of the world. The basic colour combination here is the vibrant tones of pinks, oranges and purples with gold accents. If this combination is too bright for your bathroom try using a similar combination but in pastel tones.

Difficulty level: moderate.

Where to apply

This two-layered stencil with its border and diamond repeat is ideally used with the border at the height of the sink, and the repeat pattern applied between the border and ceiling. It works equally well on silk and sheer fabrics, and the border would also be very attractive on a wide-framed mirror.

PREPARATION

Prime as necessary and then divide the walls into two sections at the height of the sink. Use a spirit level to ensure the dividing line is horizontal. Paint two coats of the deep lilac-pink matt emulsion below the height of the sink. Once this is dry, mask this off with painting tape and paint two coats of the lighter lilac-pink from sink height to ceiling. Once the paint is fully dry, varnish with two coats of acrylic matt varnish.

1 MARKING UP

Refer to Stencil Techniques (page 22). For the border stencil use a ruler and permanent marker to draw a straight line onto the first-layer stencil 1 cm (½") below the lower edge of the design. This will act as a registration guide to line up to the line on the wall where the two different pinks meet.

For the diamond repeat motif use the ruler and permanent marker to draw a vertical line running between each of the motifs on layer one of the stencil. Then use the spirit level and pencil to make a series of vertical registration marks down the left-hand side of the wall. Refer to Stencil Techniques (page 22).

2 POSITIONING STENCILS

Apply repositionable spray adhesive to the reverse of the border and repeat stencils.

Stick the border stencil securely to the wall, with the registration guideline on top of the line where the two different pinks meet.

Stick the repeat stencil to the wall above the border stencil so that the edge of the stencil lines up with the registration marks on the left-hand side of the wall; also use the spirit level to check that the vertical lines you have drawn are truly vertical.

3 STENCILLING FIRST COLOURS, FIRST REPEAT

Pour a little of each of the stencil colours into a divided palette or onto a paper plate.

The way of working the vibrant colour palette in this pattern motif is to select different sections of the design for each colour so there will be a section for the fuchsia and crimson pinks, a section for the orange and a section for the purple. This is then overprinted with the corresponding metallic colours. The pink colours should be prevalent, allowing the other two bright colours to blend and harmonize. You can devise your own system for this or follow the guidelines below.

4 SUGGESTED COLOUR LAYOUT FOR BORDER

Use the fuchsia and crimson pinks: on the left-hand side of the tulip shape in the pattern; to the left of the shape between the tulip motifs; for the centres of each of these two shapes; and for the S-shape and the linear shapes on the lower narrow border.

Use the orange to the right of the tulip motif: to the right of the shape between the tulip motifs, and between the S-shapes in the lower narrow border. Use the purple on the left of the inside of the tulip shape, the top of the tulip shape, the bottom of the shape between the tulip and in any spaces left on the lower narrow border.

5 REPEAT-MOTIF REFERENCE

Use the fuchsia and crimson pinks for the top half (the flowers) of each motif.

Use the orange for the bottom half (the leaves) of each motif. Use the purple 'blushed' around the edges of the flowers.

6 ADDING METALLIC COLOURS

Metallic colours are naturally transparent and have little impact when put straight onto the wall. However, when they are stencilled onto rich base colours, as here, they will immediately have a lustrous depth. Stencil the corresponding metallic pink, orange and purple colours on top of the flat colours. Then add touches of the two golds to parts of the orange areas.

7 STENCILLING REMAINING REPEATS

To reposition the border stencil for the rest of the border, make sure the guideline on the stencil is resting horizontally on the join line made by the two different pinks on the wall, as well as positioning the tulip motif at the left edge of the stencil so that it fits snugly into the last printed motif (the shape between the tulip shapes). Also ensure that there is the same amount of space between these two as there is between the motifs on the design itself.

You can either reposition the repeat stencil by eye, using the spirit level to check that it is vertical, or by using a ruler to mark up the distance between each of the pattern motifs and line up to this.

Repeat the stencilling process using first the flat colours, followed by the metallic top colour. Continue this process until the wall is covered.

8 GLITTER CENTRES

Apply repositionable spray adhesive to the reverse of the second-layer stencils for the border and repeat motifs and stick securely to the wall. Both of these stencils are easy to position by eye as they constitute the centres of the flowers and motifs for the first-layer stencils – just ensure that each shape is sitting inside its corresponding shape already printed and is not in any of the gaps.

This stencil will create the jewel-like, glittering centres to the flowers and shapes. It is done in two stages. First, use the gold stencil paint to stencil all the centres of the flowers and leaves on both the border and repeat motifs.

When this has dried, dab some of the ruby glitter paint onto your sponge and apply it directly to the stencil. To make the glitter paint stand out like little jewels apply a generous amount directly to the stencil with a small fitch brush.

Apply the ruby glitter paint to the centre of the tulip shape, the heart, the pendant shape between the tulip motifs, and the central flower in the repeat motif.

Apply the gold glitter paint to the remaining centres. Peel back the stencil to reveal the beauty of these glitter centres.

9 FINISHING

A thin gold line is applied directly to the join of the two pinks to give extra definition and a metallic accent.

Measure 7 mm (¼") up from the join line and mark it with pencil. Stick one length of low-tack masking tape onto the join line and another length on the marks you have just made. Press the tape down firmly by running your finger along each edge, brush over with matt varnish, and then apply two to three layers of gold acrylic paint using a fitch brush. Remove the tapes. Leave to dry until glitter paint has become hard, then use a rubber to remove any visible pencil marks, and brush off carefully.

The wall does not need another coat of varnish as two were applied on top of the base coat. Use a plastic rubber to remove any visible pencil marks and brush off.

The bright, sunny colours of Mediterranean interiors are captured perfectly in this simple, bold bathroom scheme, ideal for a room where you want a sense of warmth and invigoration.

Mediterranean floor

The polychromatic, primary colour palette employed here is simple, yet highly effective. Create this tile-effect floor, which emulates the brightly coloured, bold, simple patterns of thick Mediterranean ceramic tiles. Capture the floor colours in the walls for a really lively effect or complement the floor with pale, neutral walls.

Where to apply

This design works best as an all-over floor treatment. It can be applied to a wooden floor, but will be most effective on a flat surface such as MDF or hardboard. The flooring is probably best laid by a professional, but if you are keen on DIY, refer to a comprehensive DIY manual to guide you through the relevant stages. You will need to work with sheets of 4 mm (⅛") or 7 mm (¼") thick MDF or hardboard.

Difficulty level: **moderate. The stencil is easy to work with, but floors are hard work so allow plenty of time for completing the project.**

PREPARATION

On wooden floors make sure the surface is well sanded; fill any holes with a proprietary wood filler. On MDF or hardboard floors also fill any holes made by tack heads with a wood filler and use an appropriate sealant to fill the sheeting joins. Prime the floor and then apply two coats of ivory matt emulsion. Allow to dry thoroughly, and then varnish with one coat of acrylic matt varnish.

MARKING UP FOR BORDER AND CORNER STENCILS

Refer to Stencil Techniques (page 22). Use a set square to check if the line where the walls meet the floor is straight and square. Then, using the set square, ruler and pencil make a series of registration marks 5 cm (2") in from the edge of the floor around the whole room, compensating for any unevenness in the walls and using the set square to ensure 90° angles at the corners. These registration marks will act as guides for the border, corner and tile stencils so spend time getting this right.

The border and corner stencils both have a linear motif at the base of the design. Use the permanent marker to draw a line directly onto the Mylar 7 mm (¼") below this on both stencils.

1 STENCILLING CORNER MOTIF

Pour some of the warm red, sunny yellow and cobalt blue paint into a divided palette or onto a plate. Spray the back of the corner stencil with the repositionable adhesive and position the corner stencil so that the lines on the stencil line up with the registration marks on the floor.

Stencil the flower motif on the corner stencil lightly with the warm red. Then lightly dab a little blue in the centre of the flower and stencil the linear motif around the edge in blue. Go over the flower again in red and then dab yellow into the small square in the corner.

Remove the stencil and repeat the process in each corner of the room.

2 STENCILLING BORDER MOTIF

Spray the back of the border stencil with the repositionable adhesive and position so that the lines drawn on the stencil line up with the registration marks. Start the border next to the corner stencil.

Stencil the linear motif and the scallop motif in cobalt blue, the row of circles in sunny yellow and the diamonds in warm red. Blush the top of the blue scallop motif with a little red. Remove the stencil and position again. Stencil as before. Repeat this process until you get to the next corner. On the last repeat you may need to stencil only a section of the border to fit in with the corner motif. To do this, simply mask off the area you do not want to print by laying a piece of paper under the Mylar and stencil as normal. Continue until the border is complete.

3 MARKING UP AND POSITIONING FIRST TILE REPEAT

Measure 14 cm (5½") from the outside edge of the border stencil (linear motif) and make a series of registration marks to form a line inside the border all the way around the room. Use the set square to make sure that the corners are 90°. Use the permanent marker, ruler and set square to draw a square onto the Mylar around the edge of the cut-out motifs of the tile stencil.

Position the first tile repeat in the corner farthest from the door. The tiny triangle motif in the corner of the tile design should be closest to the corner stencil and the quarter-flower motif should be diagonally opposite.

4 STENCILLING FIRST TILE REPEAT

Working diagonally from the small triangle across to the quarter-flower motif, apply blue to the small triangle in the corner, the diagonal row of squares, the scalloped-lozenge shapes, and the single scallop shapes. Blush a little blue into the corner of the quarter-flower motif.

Stencil yellow to the short line of small circles, the diagonal row of larger squares, and the broken rectangles next to the quarter-flower motif. Stencil red to the three lines running diagonally across the tile, the longer row of circles, and the quarter-flower motif.

Some of the colours will naturally overprint. This adds to the ceramic glazed effect. To achieve colour intensity, overprint the colours twice.

5 TAPING UP GROUT LINES

Stick lining tape along the marks already made (see step 3 above). Then make another series of marks to make up two lines adjacent to the corner of the room by measuring 28 cm (11") from the outside edge of the first tape. When the tape is stuck down, check that the square measures 28 cm (11"); if it is smaller you have stuck the tape on the wrong side of the marks. Keep measuring and sticking down lining tape at intervals of 28 cm (11") to make up a grid covering the whole floor. The last square will probably be cut short, which is exactly what would happen on a tiled floor as well.

6 STENCILLING REMAINING REPEATS

The stencil is designed to be rotated 360°, to make up a full-pattern repeat. This in turn makes a series of square diamonds. In the center of one of these diamonds the quarter-flower motif lines up to make one large flower, in the other the repeat makes a series of concentric diamond shapes. The taped-up grid will help you position each repeat correctly. The square drawn on the stencil should fit perfectly inside the taped-up squares. Stencil the tile effect in rows, rotating the stencil 90°. Then rotate it back to the first position for the third repeat and so on. The second row you stencil will reveal the full pattern repeat.

7 APPLYING TINTED VARNISH

Tint 500 ml (17 fl oz) of acrylic matt varnish with five to six drops of raw umber tinter and mix thoroughly. Ensure the tapes are well stuck down and the surface is dust free. Varnish the whole stencilled area. Leave to dry.

8 REMOVING THE TAPES AND FINISHING

Peel back all of the tapes to reveal the crisp-edged grout lines beneath. Remove any pencil marks and wipe over the surface with a tack cloth. Finally, varnish the whole floor with two coats of acrylic eggshell floor varnish. Leave the floor varnish to harden for 48 hours.

Colour combos variations

Oriental soft blossom

This delicate mural includes restful Oriental motifs. You can use any combination of Oriental style stencils to make up the mural. Paint the wall with two coats of cream matt emulsion and acrylic matt varnish. Stencil moon – gold; blossom – lilac, cerise, pearl; boughs – pale brown, gold; bamboo – pale gold; fretwork and calligraphy motifs – lilac, cerise, gold (refer to Dolphin splashback, page 56).

Copper and silver

Here the simple combination of copper and silver creates a totally luxurious finish. The super non-absorbent surface of the copper paint is ideal for busy bathrooms, but extra care is needed in applying the paint to achieve a smooth surface. Refer to guidelines in Etched glass squares, page 52, for preparing and applying metallic paint. The contrasting silver effect is achieved by simply adding a gilded silver frame and brushed chrome fittings.

Scallop mosaic floor

This faux mosaic emulates traditional Roman floors. Prime and paint with two coats of white matt emulsion. Seal with acrylic eggshell varnish. Stipple a pale grey glaze over whole floor (refer to Calacatta marble, page 92). Make registration marks for the border. Stencil the corner and border motifs – pale grey, mid-grey, mid-blue, kingfisher blue. Add highlights – metallic blue, pearl, gold stencil paint/emulsion. Stencil the scallop motif inside the border using the same colours. Add two coats of acrylic eggshell floor varnish.

► Richly patterned walls create an opulent effect in this bathroom. This is further enhanced by the soft pinks of the floral motifs and bathroom fittings and the red wash on the lower walls. Fittings and accessories are kept to a minimum so as not to distract from the decorative features of the walls.

◄ This simple colour scheme creates a sense of light and space – the perfect setting for showing off this roll-top bath, which takes centre stage here. Further drama is created by light streaming through the large window – but even rooms without such direct light sources can be given a sense of light and space if the design and colour scheme are carefully planned.

Stencil templates

Refer to Stencil Techniques (page 22) for instructions on how to cut and apply stencils. The stencils here can also be bought pre-cut from www.hennydonovanmotif.co.uk.

Stencil designs copyright © Henny Donovan, 2003—may not be used for commercial purposes without prior permission of the author.

Level of difficulty

  Simple

  Medium difficulty

  Complex

Damask walls

pages 40–43

Enlarge by approx. 300% for size shown in project • Two-layer stencil
The above diagram indicates how to position stencil for repeats to make the overall pattern.

❀ Dolphin mosaic splashback and hand-painted tiles

pages 56–59

Enlarge by approx. 300% for size shown in project

✳ Geometric repeat

pages 88–91

Enlarge by approx. 120% for size shown in project • Two-layer stencil
The diagram to the right shows how to make up the stencil design used in
the project from the template below. Work with an even number
of squares across the design to create a continuous repeat without
needing to rotate the design.

☐ As template below

☐ Turn 90° counterclockwise

❀❀ Modern Swedish style

pages 60–63

◀ **Hand printed curtain stencil**
Enlarge by approx. 200% for size shown in project

Enlarge by approx. 400%

✳ Etched glass
squares

pages 52–55

Enlarge by approx. 150% for size
shown in project

▼ Tile stencil

✳ Leaf spatter

pages 64–67

Enlarge by approx. 200% for size shown
in project
Two-layer stencils

◄ Mirror frame
border stencil

✿ Relief shells on neutral squares

pages 72–75

Enlarge by approx. 150% for size shown in project
Two-layer stencils

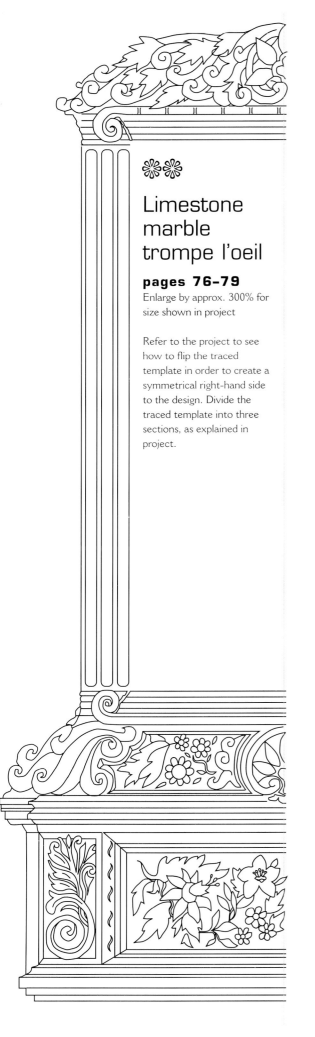

Limestone marble trompe l'oeil

pages 76–79

Enlarge by approx. 300% for size shown in project

Refer to the project to see how to flip the traced template in order to create a symmetrical right-hand side to the design. Divide the traced template into three sections, as explained in project.

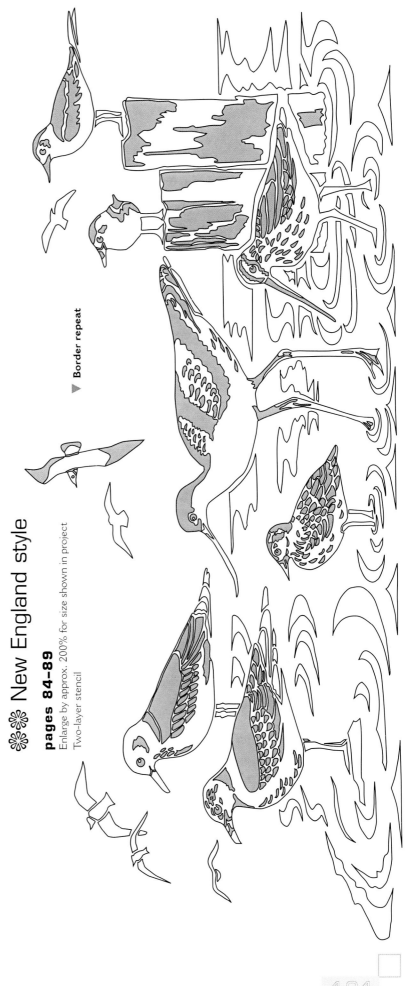

▶ Border repeat

❀ New England style

pages 84–89

Enlarge by approx. 200% for size shown in project

Two-layer stencil

◀ Border repeat

�des✹des✹des Indian style bathroom

pages 104–107

Enlarge by approx. 165% for size shown in project
Two-layer stencils

▲ **Wall motifs** ▶

6"
(15 cm)

5½"
(14 cm)

7"
(18 cm)

▲ **Guide for wall motif repeats**

▼ **Corner design for Mediterranean style**

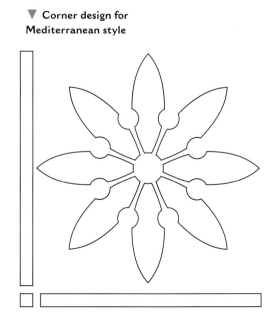

STENCIL TEMPLATES

✳ Mediterranean floor

pages 108–111

Enlarge by approx. 200% for size shown in project

▲ The floor and border repeats and the corner design are each used four times to create the Mediterranean pattern shown in the project.

◀ **Floor repeat**

▼ **Border repeat**

Resource directory

The stencils used throughout the projects in this book, designed by Henny Donovan are available at www.hennydonovanmotif.co.uk These include: Toile du Jouy, Large koi carp, Reverse feathers for etched effect, Dolphin mosaic, Reverse leaf for spattering, Wild parsley, Damask repeat, Modern shells, Geometric repeat, Shoreline border, Indian border, Indian repeat, Mediterranean tile, Dragonfly, Simple leaf, Mermaid and dolphins, Abstract oriental.

Also available: Decorative stencil paints, metallic stencil paints, glitter paints, 3-D stencil paste, porcelain paints, universal tinters, acrylic metallic varnish, acrylic varnishes, acrylic scumble glaze. Stencilling accessories, including high-density foam, specialist brushes and tapes are amongst the range of equipment available. Go to www.hennydonovanmotif.co.uk for more information.

UK

STENCIL SUPPLIERS

HENNY DONOVAN MOTIF
Website www.hennydonovanmotif.co.uk
Range of stencils used throughout this book (see above), stencil accessories, stencil paints, 3-D stencil paste, porcelain paints and varnishes. Equipment, tapes and range of brushes.

**BRUSHSTROKES
(CIRKA WALLCOVERINGS LTD)**
Ladybird House
Beeches Road
Loughborough
Leicester LE7 3NR
Tel. 01509 225280
Fax 01509 225284
Website www.cirka.uk.com
Manufacturers and retail suppliers of stencils, stamps, stencil paints, 3-D stencil paste, accessories

STENCIL CRAFT
115 Boldmere Road
Sutton Coldfield
B73 5TU
Tel. 0121 354 7070
Website www.stencil.co.uk

THE STENCIL LIBRARY
Stocksfield Hall
Stocksfield
Northumberland NE43 7TN
Tel. 01661 844844
Website www.stencil-library.com
Comprehensive catalogue of designs made to order

ARTIST'S MATERIALS AND SPECIALIST PAINTS

ATLANTIS EUROPEAN LTD
146 Brick Lane
London E1 6RU
Tel. 020 7377 8855
Fax 020 7377 8850
Mail order service available
Artist's materials, paints, and brushes

GREEN AND STONE LTD
259 Kings Road
London SW3 5EL
Tel. 020 7352 0837
Website www.greenandstone.com
Range of fine art materials, paints, brushes, stencils, gilding materials

THE JOHN JONES ART CENTRE LTD
Stroud Green Road
London N4 3JG
Tel. 020 7281 5439
Fax 020 7281 5956
Website www.johnjones.co.uk
Mail order service available
Comprehensive range of artist's materials, paints and brushes, gilding materials, stencil paints, picture frames

PEBEO (UK) LTD
For local stockists call:
Unit 416 Solent Business Centre
Millbrook Road West
Millbrook
Southampton SO15 0HW
Tel. 02380 701144
Fax 02380 901916
Website www.pebeo.com
Porcelain, tile, and glass paints, stencil paints, 3-D stencil paste, gilding materials

PLASTI-KOTE LTD
PO Box 867
Pampisford
Cambridge
CB2 4XP
Tel. 01223 836400
Fax 01223 836686
Website www.spraypaint.co.uk
Glass frosting/etching spray, brilliant metallic spray paints

E. PLOTON LTD
273 Archway Road
London N6 5AA
Tel. 020 8348 0315
Fax 0208 348 3414
Website www.ploton.co.uk
Mail order service available
Full range of artist's materials, paints and brushes, gilding materials

PAINTING, DECORATING AND DIY RETAILERS AND SUPPLIERS

J.W. BOLLOM GROUP
13 Theobald's Road
London WC1X 8FN
Tel. 020 8658 2299
Website www.bollom.com
Paints, varnishes, stains, specialist decorating equipment

C. BREWERS
327 Putney Bridge Road
London SW15 2PG
Tel. 020 8788 9335
Website www.brewers.co.uk
Decorating materials and equipment

FARROW & BALL LTD
Uddens Trading Estate
Wimborne
Dorset BH21 7NL
Tel. 0120 287 6141
Website www.farrow-ball.co.uk
Period style paints

FOXELL & JAMES LTD
57 Farringdon Road
London EC1M 3JB
Tel. 020 7405 0152
Fax 020 7405 3631
Website www.foxellandjames.co.uk
Paints, primers and range of acrylic, cellulose and polyurethane floor varnishes, Trip Trap system

PAINT MAGIC INTERIORS
61 Walcot Street
Bath
Somerset BA1 5BN
Tel. 01225 469966
Fax 01225 423040
Mail order service available. Range of emulsions, woodpaint, colourwash, impasto, stencils, stamps, stencil paint, acrylic varnishes, metallic varnish, scumble glaze

PAINTWORKS
5 Elgin Crescent
London W11 2JA
Tel. 020 7792 8012
Website www.paintworks.co.uk
Emulsions, woodpaint, colourwash, acrylic varnishes, scumble glaze

CHRIS STEVENS LTD
545-561 Holloway Road
London N19 4BT
Tel. 020 7272 1228
Trade center for paints, primers, varnish DIY materials, tiles

GLAZIERS

J. PREEDY & SONS
Stanley Works
7B Coronation Road
London NW10 7PQ
Tel. 020 8965 1323
Fax 020 8963 1281
Website www.preedyglass.com
Glass and mirror glass cut to order

TIMBER MERCHANTS, MDF SCREENS

JALI LTD
Albion Works
Church Lane
Barham
Canterbury
Kent CT4 6QS
Tel. 01227 831710
Fax 01227 831950
Website www.jali.co.uk
Mail order service available
Patterned MDF panels, grills, screens, radiator cabinets, cupboards, shelves

WM C. THOMERSON LTD
20 Middle Lane
London N8 8PL
Tel. 020 8340 2742
Fax 020 8348 2583
Website www.thomersontimber-merchants.co.uk
Full range of timber, molding and MDF, patterned MDF screens
Cutting and delivery service available

MANUFACTURERS, WHOLESALERS AND SUPPLIERS

BEDEC PRODUCTS LTD
Unit 1 and 2 Poplars Farm
Aythorpe
Roding
Nr Dunmow
Essex CM6 1RY
Website www.bedec.co.uk
Manufacturers and suppliers of emulsions, woodpaint, impasto, stencil paints, metallic and acrylic varnishes

CRAIG & ROSE PLC
172 Leith Walk
Edinburgh EH6 5EP
Tel. 0131 554 1131
Email Enquiries@craigandrose.com
Manufacturers and suppliers of emulsions, stencil paints, acrylic varnishes, scumble glaze

A. S. HANDOVER
37H Mildmay North
London N1 4RH
Tel. 020 7359 4696
Website www.handover.co.uk
Comprehensive selection of decorator's and specialist brushes, gilding materials, painting, masking and lining tape, decorating equipment

TEXTILE SUPPLIERS

Z. BUTT TEXTILES
24 Brick Lane
London E1 6RF
Tel. 020 7247 7776
Website zbutt-textiles@excite.com
Mail order service available
Fine muslins, cottons, voiles

BATHROOM SUPPLIERS

THE ALBION BATH CO
26 Hythe Quay
Colchester
Essex CO2 8JB
Tel. 07000 422847
Fax 01206 796827
Email Albionbathco@compuserve.com
Supplier of bespoke handmade baths and shower units

BATHSTORE.COM
Units 2a and b
Felnex Trading Estate
190 London Road
Hackbridge
Surrey SM6 7EL
For more information visit one of the 30 stores nationwide or telephone for brochure.
Tel. 07000 288478
Website www.bathstore.com
Baths, sinks, basins, toilets, bidets, taps, accessories

COLOURWASH
18 Weir Road
Wimbledon
London
SW19 8UG
There are 5 Colourwash showrooms in the London area.
Website www.colourwash.co.uk
Mail order service available.
Baths, sinks, basins, toilets, bidets, taps, accessories

FIRED EARTH LTD
Twyford Mill
Adderbury
Banbury
Oxfordshire OX17 3HP
Tel. 01295 821088
Fax 01295 810832
Website www.firedearth.com
Baths, sinks, basins, toilets, bidets, taps, accessories
Full range of stone, marble, terracotta floor and wall tiles
Emulsion and eggshell paints

MAIL ORDER ACCESSORIES

THE WHITE COMPANY
Unit 30
Perivale Industrial Park
Horsenden Lane South
Greenford
Middlesex UB6 7RJ
Tel. 0870 900 9555
Website www.thewhiteco.com

TOWELS AND TOILETRIES

LAURA ASHLEY HOME BY POST
Freepost
PO Box 5
Newtown
Powys SY16 1LX
Tel. 0800 868 100
Website www.lauraashley.com
Fabrics, wallpapers, home accessories, including Venetian mirrors
Emulsions and eggshell paints

NEXT DIRECTORY
PO Box 4000
Leeds LS2 8RZ
Tel. 0845 600 7000
Website www.next.co.uk
Full range of towels and bathroom accessories, cabinets, shelves, mirrors, towel rails, shower curtains, and more

USA

ARTIST'S MATERIALS AND SPECIALIST PAINTS

PEBEO OF AMERICA
Route 78
Airport Road
PO Box 714
Swanton VT 05488
Tel. (819) 829 5012
Fax (819) 821 4151
Porcelain, tile, and glass paints, stencil paints, 3-D stencil paste, gilding materials

PAINTING AND DECORATING SUPPLIERS

FARROW & BALL INC.
Tel. (845) 369 4912
Fax (845) 369 4913
E-mail usasales@farrow-ball.com
As indicated

Canada

PAINTING AND DECORATING SUPPLIERS

FARROW & BALL
1054 Yonge Street
Toronto
Ontario
Tel. (416) 920 0200
Fax (416) 920 1223
E-mail fandb@istar.com
As indicated

Australia

PAINTING AND DECORATING SUPPLIERS

LIBERON WAXES LTD
Stoneleigh Gallery
1A Darley Street
Darlinghurst
N.S.W. 2010
Tel. (61) 2 93607780
Fax (61) 2 93607798
Shellac, waxes, metallic creams

New Zealand

PAINTING AND DECORATING SUPPLIERS

DAVE MORRISON FURNITURE
271 Ferry Road
Christchurch
Tel. (64) 03 389 8288
Fax (64) 03 389 8288
Shellac, waxes, metallic creams

Index

Credits

Author acknowledgements and thanks:

Keith Bourdice for tireless support, encouragement and help with set painting and construction. **Zoe Miller** for meticulous proofing and help with set painting. **Paul Forrester** and **Colin Bowling** for photography. **Sally Bond** for art editing and help putting my set designs together. **Kate Tuckett** for editing, project management, and sourcing props. **Jan Cutler** for copyediting. **Nikki Linton** for product sourcing. **Harriet Merry** for picture sourcing. **Sheila Volpe** for assistance with Damask stencilling.

The author and Quarto would like to thank the following companies for supplying props and supplies for photography:

Paint Magic Interiors for paints and varnishes used throughout the book

Brushstrokes (Cirka Wallcoverings) for Mylar and stencil paint used throughout the book

Bedec Products for specialist metallic emulsion

Pebeo Ltd for porcelain paints, stencil paints, gilding materials and stencil paste

John Jones for artist's materials and frames

Plasti-kote for etching/frosting spray and silver brilliant metallic spray paint

Wm C Thomerson for discounts on timber, moulding and MDF, and for cutting all shapes and sizes

Fired Earth for loan of Bain de Bateau bath (p. 63 and cover) and Corinthian Stone Bowl (p. 79)

Bathstore.com for loan of taps used throughout, Calla frosted glass bowl with 600mm glass top (p. 35), bath and bath panel (pp. 39, 111), chrome shower head, chrome shower rail (p. 47), chrome towel rail (pp. 47, 75), chrome gallery shelf (p. 75), Muirfield I hole basin (p. 67), chrome gallery shelf (p. 67), Zero trough basin with chrome wrack soap dish (pp. 59, 95), chrome extendable bath rack (p. 85), Guido stainless steel basin (p. 91)

Colourwash for loan of cone basin (pp. 43, 87, 103)

Laura Ashley for loan of Venetian mirror (p. 43)

Next Mail Order for loan of glass shelves floor unit (p. 57) and round aluminium mirror (p. 55)

The White Co. for loan of towels and bathroom accessories used throughout the book.

Quarto would like to acknowledge and thank the following for supplying pictures reproduced in this book (key: l left, r right, c centre, t top, b bottom): p. 6bl The Amtico Company Ltd. (www.amtico.com); p. 7tc The Dulux Media Centre at Ketchum, bathroom featured is Spanish Bathroom—BA2-WC (weww.ketchum.com); p. 8tl Fired Earth Ltd. (www.firedearth.com); p.11tc Utopia Furniture Ltd. (24-hour brochure line +44 1902 406405 or visit the website at www.utopiagroup.com); p. 24tl Utopia Furniture Ltd.; p. 28tl Albion Bath Co. (www.albionbathco.co.uk),tc Fired Earth Ltd., lc Fired Earth Ltd., rc Albion Bath Co., br Fired Earth Ltd.; p. 29tl Albion Bath Co., tc Fired Earth Ltd., tr Fired Earth Ltd., c Albion Bath Co.; p. 8lt Utopia Furniture Ltd., b The Amtico Company Ltd.; p. 97t HK Art Projects (www.hkartprojects.co.uk), b Fired Earth Ltd.; p. 113 Susie Gradwell, b Abode Interiors Photography and Library (www.abodepix.co.uk);